Democritus University of Thrace

Jacques Lacan
An Introduction to his Psychoanalysis

Eleni Boliaki

P.M.P. Paschalidis
Medical Publications

PMP (Paschalidis Medical Publications, Ltd.).
14th, Tetrapoleos str., Athens, 115 27, Greece
Tel.: 003-210-7789125, 003-210-7793012, Fax: 003-210-7759421,
e-mail: Paschalidis@Medical-Books.gr
orders: Paschalidis@Medical-Books.gr
© information: GP@Medical-Books.gr, CP@Medical-Books.gr

ISBN: 960-399-512-6

9 789603 995128

JACQUES LACAN: AN INTRODUCTION TO HIS PSYCHOANALYSIS

Contents

Introduction

Lacan was a reminder of something fundamental. He examined human nature and human condition against any narrowly defined parameters and claimed ignorance of the self, which does not exist as a constitution, as a sum of attitudes revolving around a core, but, instead, as a borderland: it is not a stable, recognizable entity, but an open field of outside forces, false identifications, and self-deceptions, it is a fusion of inside and outside, a collage, a collection of partial views. For Lacan, there is a fundamental inadequacy--internal and integral--a biological insufficiency, a lack of being, a lack of ontological autonomy, an ontological uncertainty on which suffering is founded and which marks the ultimate tragedy of the human condition. Because one lacks innate being and wants to eradicate this loss, one identifies with persons and images, while the ego is this internalization of otherness. His consequent acknowledgment that human wanting exceeds being makes him tragic.[1]

Lacan focused on the power of (self) deception and one's systematic misrecognition of reality. He, indeed, understood madness as this misrecognition, as *meconnaissance,* the lack of any distinct border between reality and illusion, truth and imagination, self and other. He also understood that madness could not be eradicated

---

[1] As Marshall W. Alcorn Jr. says, "Lacan's subject is perhaps best defined as the one who suffers ... the drama of the subject." Marshall W. Alcorn Jr., "The Subject of Discourse," in *Lacanian Theory of Discourse,* ed. Bacher, M., Marshall W. Alcorn Jr., Ronald J. Corthell, and Francoise Massardier-Kenney, New York: New York University Press, 1994, p. 28.

precisely because it is founded on *meconnaissance,* the original insanity, that is, the imaginary relation to the world, that pathology that structures human development. Madness is a permanent dimension of human psyche, an integral part of human personality, universal, interracial, interethnic. Standing against enforced rules on sanity, he thus subverted the conventional boundaries between normality and pathology and doubted that sanity and insanity are incompatible; by pathologizing normalcy Lacan normalized pathology and humanized madness. He also stressed that both madness and health are rhetorics that make arbitrary definitions based on assumptions about specific social values, and that they are social products to be interrogated.

Lacan reevaluated and renewed some questions, aspired to transform thinking, and opposed any views that today would be part of positivism, which reduces all knowledge to statements that are certain, and truth to the correspondence of thoughts to things. For him, there exists no ultimate and invariable standard for truth, and all thought remains provisional. Along with his wondering about what it means to be human and his fundamental insights into the human psyche, he also doubted one's ability to exhaust or reduce anything to any single analysis, for, human experience, as the product of forces which are plural and relational as well as out of control, cannot be explained or defined by constraining categories. The work of Lacan resists any final systematization, since there are limits and uncertainties in the fields of knowledge. In a world in which nothing is fixed, confirmed or settled, there is nothing permanent, not even the true. Certainty and objectivity are impossible, and everything said is rhetoric, since knowledge is imperfect and language never expresses something completely--it does not represent any signified, but only another signifier. Knowledge provides a partial representation of things, it is always a partial view, an inclination, a speculation; the analysand will decide the meanings. This is also what makes him tragic: his continuously suspended, precarious meanings, the meaninglessness of meaning, that is, the confrontation with death, with nothingness. For him there is no home to call one's own.

Not pleased with a brute reality, Lacan nonetheless advocated a "willing suspension of disbelief," the state in which one is not deluding oneself that one is not deluded. To be human and mature is to live with reality's ambiguities and to be aware and recognize self-delusion. Here, analysis provides the awareness that may lead to such a reflective life--an end in itself.

Context

Lacan lived in times of social change, of collapsing worlds, cultural decay and widespread moral anarchy. He lived after the Great War which itself marked the collapse of French society and a dissolution of the boundaries between normal and pathological. The attempt for a just and caring world had failed.

Carolyn Dean, in her book *The Self and its Pleasures,* demonstrates how theory and history are implicated in each other, how theory represents, symbolizes, and hence constructs history and vice versa. She examines the time and place of the specific theory of self dissolution in psychoanalysis, and contextualizes and historisizes Lacan's historically and culturally specific and symptomatic theory of the decentered self. She locates it in a cultural crisis in interwar France in which all the criteria defining what makes a self and what gives it legitimacy were perceived as having dissolved, and traces Lacan's revision of Freud to the efforts to rehabilitate criminals in interwar France.[2] The criminal is a metaphor for an other self that the mental hygiene movement, the French psychoanalysts, and the surrealists tried to rescue, paradoxically causing the dissolution of this other self.

Lacan was both a critique and protester of centers of power and control, against the social and psychiatric imperialisms that imposed

---

[2]C. J. Dean, The Self and Its Pleasures: Bataille, Lacan, and the History of the Decentered Subject, Ithaca and London: Cornell University Press, 1992, p. 3.

norms of rationality and let the strong dominate the weak.[3] In France, after about 1860, constitutionalism referred to a physical rather than a mental predisposition to mental illness according to which the physique, along with the behavior of the criminal, was the locus and the evidence of the deviance. The psychiatrists conceived criminals as the transparent expressions of a deviant soul and, according to them, the "degenerates" were inadequately adapted organisms. Dean claims that, in a period of labor unrest, the intention behind the harsh punishment was not medical but political,[4] and that the legislators exploited the psychiatric language in order to justify harsh penalties, including the capital punishment and the Relegation Act of 1885. As soon as psychiatrists received more power after World War I and became part of the national endeavor to regenerate French morals, they supported the replacement of legal with medical diagnosis of the criminal based on the advances of psychiatry. And while French courts judged criminal responsibility according to a classical conception of free will, the psychiatrists' main task was to decide whether the delinquent was sane or insane, that is, whether the criminal could be held legally responsible for the crime or not. It was not the nature of the crime, but the perversity of the doer that would determine the punishment.

Although psychiatrists were the ones who would define who was a criminal or not, they, ironically, found themselves unable to penetrate into the criminal and to draw the line between sanity and insanity:

---

[3]On this, one may recall Thomas Szasz, who in his book, *The Manufacture of Madness,* talks about the 'messianic' psychiatry: "The fundamental conflicts in human life are not between competing ideas, one "true" and the other "false"--but rather between those who hold power and use it to oppress others, and those who are oppressed by power and seek to free themselves of it." T. Szasz, The Manufacture of Madness, Dell, 1970, p. 63.

[4]Dean, p. 17-8.

"The increasing medicalization of deviance brought about a greater reliance on psychiatric expertise and yet also revealed its fallibility."[5] Faced with the discrepancy between pathological behavior (clinical symptoms) and psychic motivation (diagnosis of pathology), that is, the "ego's" participation in the criminal act, psychiatrists realized that the epistemological foundations of positivist analysis could not explain crimes that were apparently unmotivated. Only an unconscious process could explain it. But then, they confronted criminals who had no control of their unconscious, who were not responsible, yet they were normal. Consequently, there was a confusion about who should be rehabilitated and how.

For Lacan, only psychoanalysis could demonstrate the relationship between the causes and the symptoms. Along with the odd behavior, he saw the disordered speech as the symptom of psychosis. What fascinated the young Lacan were those discrepancies between a criminal's words and his actions or his writing.[6] He discerned that the structures of language play a role in the mechanisms issuing in the irruption of the unconscious, an effect that has a complex causality, and, thus, he recognized language as a clue to a mental state. He discerned the connection between psychosis and confused language and, studying the language of madness, he expressed his total rejection of constitutionalism.

According to Dean, Lacan's primary insight in Freud's topography is the concept of the pathology of autopunition, a self-punishment, a "satisfaction which is the opposite of a satisfaction,"[7] based on which he explained the ego formation and defined the structure of human

---

[5]Dean, p. 32.

[6]Ibid., p. 27.

[7]Jacques Lacan, <u>The Seminar of J. Lacan: Book II: The Ego in Freud's Theory and in the Technique of Psychoanalysis, 1954-55,</u> ed. Jacques-Alain Miller, New York: W. W. Norton, 1988, p. 212-3.

motivation. In 1932, in his medical thesis *De la Psychose paranoïaque dans ses rapport avec la personalitè,* Lacan attempted to understand what motivated Aimée, a woman with no obvious reason, to try to murder an actress she had never personally met. He reexamined Freud's concept of the ego, claiming that the reality principle is in no way separable from the pleasure principle,[8] and that the ego is not clearly differentiated from the id, and redefined the self's structure in terms of a repression that is always a pleasure. By correlating reality and pleasure, Lacan implied that there is a pathology (autopunition) always structured in the normal self, and used Aimée as a metaphor for a permanent dimension of the human psyche and ego that is always an illusion trapped within the mirrors of its own making. Aimée transformed a paranoid demand for satisfaction into a self-punishment paranoia.[9] Paradoxically, the crime is a form of pathology that is also always a cure, a liberation from guilt that sustains the desire to be guilty:

> And, after all, wasn't it Freud who introduced the function of the libido into human behavior? ... people seek their pleasure. So, why is this expressed theoretically by a principle which states the following--what is sought is, in the end, the cessation of pleasure... in the pleasure principle, pleasure, by definition, is bent to its end... is that pleasure should cease... the reality principle consists in making the game last... in ensuring that pleasure is renewed....[10]

The self "exists" the moment of the crime-autopunition, which at the same time is a punishment for non-existing. Self-punishment

---

[8]Jacques Lacan, <u>De La Psychose paranoïaque dans ses rapports avec la person-alitè</u>, Paris: Seuil, 1975, p. 324.
[9]Ibid., p. 253, 265.
[10]Lacan, <u>Book II</u>, p. 84.

affirms and structures the self: "the *passage à l'acte* is the moment when an unconscious drive to self-punishment paradoxically gives the self its form, when the desire to be an other whom one cannot be is satisfied because unsatisfied, repressed... the self can be known only when it is repressed...."[11]

According to Lacan, the nature of the cure reveals the nature of the disease. By striking at the actress, Aimée was striking at her own ideal self: "Aimée's crime dramatizes the tragic human struggle to be free of others, whose recognition human beings always desire: the struggle to be free of the mirrors that are at once the source of human slavery and human pleasure."[12] Later, Lacan would argue more openly that the motive behind the crime is autopunition, the desire to be guilty, and that guilt is constitutive of the subject.

Subsequently, while a criminal act can reveal that the self is an illusion, the "motivation" behind a crime is an incurable madness. It is not symbolic of one's unconscious, of a hidden self to be discovered --for, the "true", hidden self does not exist--but of a self whose truth cannot be represented because it is perpetually displaced. The core of one's being is always someplace else. The unconscious is the deviant within and Aimée is the metaphor of the criminal who dissolves the boundaries between the normal and the pathological.

In this way Lacan subverted the conventional boundaries between normality and pathology, or, put in another way, he normalized pathology. There is no such thing as sanity. As a consequence, as Mark Taylor says, "... if lack is "original" and not secondary, then it is not necessarily a deficiency. Furthermore, if lack entails no deficiency, one might become free of the dreadful need to overcome it."[13] As all are fundamentally pathological, in the same way, the psychotic is human.

---

[11]Dean, p. 57.
[12]Ibid., p. 51-2.

By normalizing pathology, Lacan humanized psychotics. Understanding madness not as a rupture of the orders of consciousness, as an other, he made it an integral part of human personality. Psychosis is not a primitive phenomenon but universal, interracial, interethnic. The deviant, psychotic and criminal, symbolize what cannot be known; they structure a lack at the heart of knowledge, they become the metaphor of the self whose actions are driven by illusions. For Lacan, there is no relationship between paranoid psychosis and the self: they are the same thing. Madness is not evidence of an ailing mind but of an incurable, hopeless self: "Madness, far from been an accident befalling an organism because of its frailties, is the permanent virtuality of a rift opened in its very essence."[14] The discordance and disturbance of harmony and equilibrium are not "somewhere" in the individual, they are everywhere and totalizing. The cogito itself includes madness.

In madness, there may be a difference in degree but not in nature. This difference may refer to an excitation, a deviation, a deficiency or excess, an irritation, a disturbance. Excess in everything may be viewed as a defect or deprivation. As Georges Canguilhem claims, "the pathological phenomena found in living organisms are nothing more than quantitative variations," and "... semantically, the pathological is designated as departing from the normal not so much by a- or -dys as by hyper- or hypo-."[15] However, the terms used are vaguely quantitative, still having a qualitative resonance, for, inasmuch as quantity refers to increase, decrease and diminution, it implies both homogeneity and variation. Don't quantitative differences have quali-

---

[13]M. C. Taylor, Erring: A Postmodern A/theology, Chicago: The University of Chicago Press, 1984, p. 14.

[14]J. Lacan, Écrits: A Selection, Trans. Alan Sheridan, New York: W.W. Norton, 1997, p. 176.

[15]Georges Canguilhem, The Normal and the Pathological, trans. Carolyn R. Fawcett, New York: Zone Books, 1989, p. 42.

tatively different effects, since alteration can also be qualitative? Madness is not simply a disorder of a corresponding normal function but an ontological affect, and one cannot perceive the transition from the normal to the pathological state precisely because there is an intimate fusion. Since there may be a homogeneity, the pathological does not differ from the normal as one quality differs from another. Furthermore, even if there is heterogeneity, one's efforts cannot restore the norms and modify the qualities. It is, therefore, not a matter of degree but of complexity.

One may infer that, according to the above, all people are potential criminals, having criminal qualities that differ quantitatively, having different degrees at different times.

Ego Psychology and Behaviorism

The partisan conflict among the circles of psychology and psycho-analysis has been about concepts as well as methods, which have been mainly based on different conceptions of the nature of illness and which suggest different requirements for recovery and therapy. Lacan's understanding of human nature and madness in particular could be explained by the context within which he worked which is mainly defined by his opposition to the methods of Behavior Therapy and Ego Psychology. These two presume the existence of a given-in-advance, neutral "external reality", an entity independent of the subject, the latter being a sum of attitudes revolving around a core, an essence that may be disintegrated and reintegrated. The investigation of the context against which Lacan worked will make it clear why he insisted that intellectual reason or rational intellect and sceptical consciousness are not the primary agents of the human mind, which is rather a bricolage of multiple agents whose organization is shifting and occasional. Lacan opposed these methods, he desubstantialized the subject and constructed the foundations of a new conception of subjectivity with the unconscious implying a radical alterity.

1. "Behavior therapy" or Conditioning therapy:

While psychoanalysis deals with inner forces of behavior and their interpretation, behaviorism emphasizes biological heritage and deals with observable activities and environmental events. The behaviorist starts with the axiom that "understanding the pathological begins with the study of physiology."[16] Asserting that self-knowledge is not important, the behaviorist underestimates the power of one's past and claims that its reawakening brings suffering which is not only unnecessary but also cruel. Behaviorism is concerned more with conditioning than with inner and primary processes and claims that one cannot be sure--since one cannot prove it scientifically--that there are internal events of which one is not conscious.

A psychology developed in laboratories, behavior therapy is a procedure for relieving distress by altering the behavior. According to it, getting rid of the symptom removes the conflicts and cures the neurosis, since behavior is not just a symptom, but all there is. As long as outward behavior is normal, one is conceived to be well adjusted. Allegedly, the primary criterion is the well-being of the patient and the quick, complete and enduring alleviation of suffering: the symptoms improve; there is an increase in productiveness, improved interpersonal relationships, general improvement of adjustment, and ability to handle ordinary psychological conflicts. The therapist need not put too much effort, and the cost the patient has to afford is the minimum. As Cyril M. Franks says, "It can be applied to the unsophisticated, the uneducated, the primitive, the dull, and even to the stranger in our midst who knows no tongue other than his own."[17]

On the basis of experimental and clinical evidence, behavioral therapy claims that neuroses are unadaptive habits that have been conditioned and learned, the result of external rather than internal forces. Maladjustment is malconditioning and, therefore, a learning

---

[16]The Conditioning Therapies: a Challenge in Psychotherapy, ed. J. Wolpe, A. Salter and L. J. Reyna, Holt, Rinehart and Winston Inc., 1964, p. v.
[17]Cyril. M. Franks, "Individual Differences in Conditioning," in The Conditioning Therapies, p. 163.

process. Even anxiety is perceived as a habit: "Human emotional problems are the result of personal miseducation. It (conditioned reflex therapy) believed that only by learning new emotional habits could the neurotic individual learn to be happy."[18] Everything that can be learned can also be unlearned and the cure consists of the reverse direction of unlearning, of undoing the undesirable patterns. Since for behaviorism the only teacher is experience and the individual's problems are the result of his or her social experiences, and since there is no underlying, inner and hidden psychical disease which creates symptoms but only external conditions, it takes the external circumstances into serious account. The patient should be retrieved from the mercy of the environment in which the therapist finds him or her, an unhealthy situation that is impossible to overcome. The therapist has first of all to identify the conditions that control the unwanted behavior and then try to change them by altering the environment and by taking the patient away from any chronic and disturbing enemy. By a simple reorienting and refocusing of one's techniques of social relations, one can change his or her personality: "The solution of all problems of the self comes from unbraking the individual's behavior with other people."[19]

Based on the work of Pavlov, this reconditioning therapy grants to speech an important role. Its method depends on the "verbal chemistry", that is, the transmission of the words spoken by the therapist to the patient through nerve tracts. These words produce chemical modifications in the patient's nervous system that are associated with behavior changes which, in their turn, induce more chemical changes.[20] Speech, thus, becomes the motor, the powerful

---

[18]A. Salter, "The Theory and Practice of Conditioned Reflex Therapy," in The Conditioning Therapies, p. 21.

[19]Ibid., p. 24.

[20]Salter, p. 24.

impact on the way one's mental processes are organized. By and through speech, in this way, one can modify the environment that influences him or her so that it does not have the effect it had before.

Lacan showed not simply disinterest but contempt to symptomatic recovery of this kind. He was interested in radical and lasting personality change that would result in the freedom from symptoms. He considered behavior therapies naive and a caricature of scientific method, a technique and not an art. With this method of behavioral psychology and the application of results from experiments with animals on human individuals, there is a lapse in an anthropomorphism in reverse and one should wonder if the method of Pavlov should be applied to human beings who have a more complex cerebral cortex. Lacan thinks that,

> There is a radical difference between any investigation of human beings, even in the laboratory, and what happens in animals. On the animal side, one shifts within a fundamental ambiguity between instinct and learning... animal learning displays the characteristics of an organized and finite mode of becoming perfect. How different it is from what the same research... reveals about learning in man!... In man it is the wrong form which prevails. In so far as a task is not completed, the subject returns to it.... But it is not enough to measure, one must also try to understand.[21]

For Lacan, one's behavior is not all one is. Behaviorism is naive in its overestimation of the effectiveness of habits and has an exaggerated interest in symptomatic recovery. It is a "superficial

---

[21]Lacan, Book II, p. 85-6.

character analysis," since its outcome is temporary with superficial results, and the symptom removal it professes is always followed by symptom substitution.

Yet, one cannot deny that one can be conditioned and un- or re-conditioned. But the conditioning therapy can turn one into a slave. If the claim of the "verbal chemistry" is true, and words spoken by the therapist travel along appropriate nerve tracts in the patient and produce chemical modifications in his or her nervous system,[22] in conditioned therapy speech has an obvious suggestive or "hypnotic" quality, which points to the acceptance of the existing values and of what is perceived as reality. Brainwashing is another word to describe what the therapist tries to do by shaping the patient's behavior. The therapist, who sets a stimulus (cause) that enforces a certain effect, has too much influence by suggestion. As Lacan says, "The order created by Freud demonstrates that the axial reality of the subject isn't in his ego. Intervening by substituting oneself for the ego of the subject... is suggestion, not analysis."[23] By practicing this method of the manipulation of behavior, the therapist becomes the "conditioner" who specifies in advance the response of the patient and tries to maneuver his or her behavior towards that direction. By rewards--called "positive reinforcement"--the therapist increases the probability for the recurrence of predetermined responses and one can control the behavior one is trying to achieve on the patient and predict the result of the therapy. The "faith", however, that the patient must have in the therapist is a conditioned effect and one becomes easily aware of the (un)ethical, religious, political and so forth, consequences this might have.

---

[22] Ibid., p. 25.
[23] Lacan, Book II, p. 43.

2. Ego Psychology

Between the thirties and the fifties, when Lacan rekindled an interest in Freud and developed his style, the Second World War demanded that many reorient themselves in a world of renewed absurdity, and here is where Lacan saw the defense mechanisms at their best... or worst. Along with thousands of immigrants, Freudian analysis was taken from Europe to America, and, in the same way that many newcomers denied their traumatic past, psychoanalysis distorted and denied Freud's interpretations. Lacan saw Freud's insights practiced not to cure but to defend from a devastating recognition of the absence of an incorruptible worldview. The newcomers needed a self and many ideals, at least the same ones that saved them from the war and brought them with hopes to America. Although their strong defenses betrayed a lack of trust, their attitude might be regarded as an instinctive resistance to anything tragic, and not an immature regression. As a rule for survival, they *had* to recognize the new reality and adapt to it. Similar to them, Freudian psychoanalysis--relocated and *emigré,* a resident alien[24]--had to adapt, too, and remove the spirit of subversion that Lacan would, later, try to rekindle.

According to Ego Psychology, the self exists as a constitution, as a sum of attitudes revolving around a core, an essence that may be disintegrated and reintegrated. The ego, both bodily and mentally, is viewed as a synthesizing, structuring system that contains "a whole organization of certainties, beliefs, of coordinates, of references."[25] In

---

[24]S. Shamdasani, "Introduction: The Censure of the Speculative," in Speculations After Freud: Psychoanalysis, Philosophy and Culture, ed. Sonu Shamdasani and Michael Munchow, New York: Routledge, 1994, p. xiii.
[25]J. Lacan, The Seminar of Jacques Lacan: Book I: Freud's Papers on Technique, 1953- 1954. ed. J.-Alain Miller, New York: Norton, 1988, p. 23.

fact, it contains knowledge. It is itself consciousness, that is, it is the organ of perception, attention and logical thinking.[26] Ego psychology is based on a commonsensical approach which also accepts the existence of a given in advance, neutral "external reality", an entity independent of the subject, and all the psychological problems and their solutions are reduced to the degree of one's adjustment to this reality. The "normal" individual is the one capable of properly connecting, accommodating and conforming to it and blindly submitting to its authorities. Ego psychology sees a discord between the reality principle which, from without, exerts its pressures and disturbs the established harmony, and the pleasure principle. In order to be "normal" one should be willing to exchange enjoyment for the reality principle. Through its devices of defense mechanisms that deal with external and internal realities, the ego protects the boundaries between these two.

According to ego psychologists, the ego undergoes continuous changes in quality and intensity. In psychoses there is a breaking down of the sense of reality and an impairment, an impoverishment of the ego and its functions which have lost interest in the external world: "The basis of sanity is correct and automatic recognition of this breach between subjective mental individual experiences in the world and the knowledge of the status of the world as it actually exists (sic): Sanity means dealing with the world and with oneself with the faculty of distinguishing clearly between them."[27] The ego's boundaries separate the external reality from the inner mentality. But these boundaries are flexible. When the ego is healthy, repressed

---

[26]G. Bychowski, Psychotherapy of Psychosis, New York: Grune & Stratton, 1952, p. 195.

[27]P. Federn, Ego Psychology and the Psychoses, New York: Basic Books Inc., 1952, p. 229.

material does not reach it. When the ego is highly developed and organized and its cathexis is strong, it is able to bring unity and coherence, and thus, it can postpone or renounce a gratification and resist frustration.

The psychotic, on the other hand, is characterized by the inability to maintain adequate demarcations between reality and pleasure. The psychotic has suffered from reality and does not want to return to it. He or she resists, shuts off and denies the external reality, and builds a distorted world of his or her own. It can also be there is a fluidity of ego boundaries and an inability to discriminate from the outside world. When the inner ego boundary gets weak and deficient, then the ego cathexis is withdrawn and one feels emotional strain, discomfort and estrangement, that is, loss of reality, because resistance is diminished and the defenses fail to maintain repression. The core of psychosis is a weak ego that fails in its basic synthetic functions. It is caught in an ambivalence and a tendency to disintegrate and regress to an undifferentiated stage in which parts of the ego find themselves in the outside world and parts of the outside reality are experienced as belonging to the ego. Poorly differentiating from the nonego, it is unable to master and control the instincts and to integrate experiences, impulses and aims. When the ego is ill, one creates false realities, delusions that are experienced as real, and one becomes unable to utilize a controlled conceptual thinking. Reality loses its importance and one is rather exposed to the invasion of the unconscious, becoming the prey of illusions. One ends up living with a strange and inappropriate behavior that produces alienation from the reality of one's ego.

According to the ego psychology's view of mental illness (e.g., psychosis and paranoia), the therapist can not only explain it but she or he can also cure it. The goal is to reconstruct the personality and to adjust it to reality. Normal means realistic and adulthood and maturation occurs when the ego solidifies its boundaries. To cure the primary symptom, the confusion between thought and reality, one must develop the sense of reality by no longer repressing the reality control and by strengthening the ego. This implies the recognition of reality's constant independence and the systematic confrontation of the ego with it, that is, the outside world, which is an entirely distinct and separate sphere. Since, according to some ego psychologists, the world of psychotics is an unrealistic, archaic, prelogical, primitive one,[28] and since the pleasure principle dominated the mental life of the primitive who must yield to the principle of reality in order to get civilized, in the same way--since one cannot direct reality according to one's wishes, although hard to renounce them--the psychotic should become aware and repress his or her desires, and adjust and com-promise. When the ego constitutes itself by organizing and integrating impulses, it ostracizes the Lacanian Real.[29] Through analysis, which focuses on the interpretation of defense mechanisms, one explores one's irrational behavior, assesses the resistances, produces insights into one's instinctual drives and, thus, relieves anxiety. The psychotic, who cannot tolerate frustration and deprivation, and whose repressed unconscious overflows the conscious ego, should re-repress the repressed unconscious.[30]

[handwritten margin note: The goal of ego psychology]

According to that, the pointing out and appeasing of the conflicts and the defense against them is a self-healing process. However, the role of the analyst is crucial. Not only should he or she express a direct affection, interest and sympathy, but also his or her role is imperative in the strengthening of the patient's ego. The identification with the analyst is what strengthens one's ego. As Bychowski claims, "The weak ego of the patient receives help from the "transfusion" coming from the ego of the therapist."[31] Since sympathy is based on the capacity for

---

[28]Federn, p. 2.

[29]On the *Real* see page 32.

[30]Federn, p. 170.

[31]Federn, p. 168.

identification and the merging of boundaries, and since, therefore, one can not sympathize with a psychotic without losing one's sanity, the ego psychologists expect that the therapist must have a strong ego himself or herself: "We need a certain amount of narcissism to appreciate the value of what we are doing and to maintain the integrity of our ego."[32]

There have been several variations within the circle of ego psychologists. One of them is that of P. Federn who equates the ego with the actual sensation, the *feeling* of one's own ego, and states that the ego is an *Erlebnis,* a subjective experience.[33] This *ego feeling* is the continuous mental experience and apprehension of unity, continuity in time and space, as well as causality of the individual's mental and bodily life, and not the integrative function of the mind: "*Ego feeling,* then, is the totality of feeling which one has of one's own living person.... *Ego feeling...* is produced in the personality by the fact of its own existence...."[34] The Cartesian *Cogito ergo sum* is assumed and it implies that "feeling my ego proves to me that thinking and being are mine."[35] Federn, however, distinguishes consciousness from *ego feeling,* the latter being the permanent entity of self-experience and the bearer as well as the object of consciousness. The ego is subject and object at the same time, it knows itself and observes itself. One is conscious of one's ego, although, as long as the ego functions normally, one is not aware of it.

This *ego feeling* proves the existence of the ego that is not a concept or an abstraction, but an entity, the core of any living individual. Even emotions are an ego function. The ego is a distinct entity opposed to the external reality that is self-evident and it is "subject to no further test."[36] For Federn, everything that is real is

---

[32]Ibid., p. 155.

[33]Ibid., p. 5.

[34]Ibid., p. 62.

[35]Ibid., p. 212.

[36]Ibid., p. 96.

also certain. Reality and certainty are tested as well as directly felt, although one individual cannot prove them and the consensus of other persons is necessary.[37]

According to Federn, in the formation of psychoses there are ambivalent emotional tendencies that tear the ego into separate, non-united parts, thus the term schizophrenia expresses the defeat of the ego by the ego-alien impulses. What cause ego weakening are the identifications that use up ego cathexis.[38] The schizophrenic's ego boundaries are weak and deficient, and as a result, there is a fusion of an estranged and an actual reality.

The cure consists in enriching and restoring the ego cathexis by reestablishing, strengthening and enlarging the ego and its resistance, and the producing of repressions. Again, one has to proceed to a hygiene of the ego: "The cure itself is accomplished by finding and appeasing the instinctual and emotional conflicts which have caused the withdrawal of ego cathexis."[39] Thus, any attempt for adaptation and maturation necessitates an increase of the ego cathexis. Any claim from the unconscious must be hindered, and, "so far as possible the patient must be released from responsibilities." At this point Federn makes the distinction between psychoses and neuroses, the latter expressing the ego's defense against ego-alien impulses: *"In neuroses, we want to lift repression; in psychoses, we want to create re-repression."*[40] Unlike neuroses, psychoses are not a defense, but a defeat.[41]

---

[37]Ibid., p. 232.

[38]Later, however, he would say that what causes the deficient supply is not known. He would admit that no one knows the nature of the pathogeny itself.

[39]Federn, p. 162.

[40]Ibid., p. 136.

[41]Ibid., p. 188.

As in behaviorism, in order to re-establish resistance, one of the things ego therapy has to do is to abandon free association: "It is imperative not to take the anamnesis, the history of a psychotic patient, since the memories of former psychotic episodes may produce a relapse."[42] The abandonment of the analysis of resistance that maintains repression is not sanctioned, for, it "is not desirable to free more repressed material and more primary processes. The analyst's responsibility forbids his making the patient more psychotic."[43] Federn concludes: "Therefore it is well to repeat our introductory principle: With neurotics our aim is to make the unconscious conscious, with psychotics to make the conscious unconscious again."[44]

One notices that the therapist on this view becomes a hygienist. His or her task is to strengthen and reintegrate, to heal the patient's weakened ego boundary, make him or her aware of the false realities, and recognize the evident outer reality as it is really perceived. Indeed, one's role as therapist is to preserve his or her influence by nourishing the positive transference that should never be resolved by psychoanalysis, for, the new identification with the analyst strengthens the patient's ego.[45] The patient should be aided and protected[46] but

---

[42]Ibid., p. 21.

[43]Ibid., p. 155. Lacan has a very different opinion. In *Écrits* he asserts that "... one is not cured because one remembers. One remembers because one is cured." p. 260.

[44]Ibid., p. 178.

[45]Although Federn sees the need of transference as permanent, he also sees the need for a favorable and helpful environment and a community of supporters, acknowledging the importance of others (siblings or friends) who would show their love and care for the patient.

[46]Federn, p. 120.

also willing to obey.[47] It becomes obvious that, as R. E. Sullivan observes, resistance comes from the analyst, not from the analysand.[48] America was a fertile field for the Ego Psychology that, according to Lacan, was the betrayal of Freudian Psychoanalysis, but also part of a struggle for survival:

> By persisting in describing the nature of resistance as a permanent emotional state, thus making it alien to the discourse, today's psychoanalysts have simply shown that they have fallen under the blow of one of the fundamental truths that Freud rediscovered through psychoanalysis. One is never happy making way for a new truth, for it always means making our way into it: the truth is always disturbing. We cannot even manage to get used to it. We are used to the real. The truth we repress.[49]

Ego-psychology, by applying a pseudo-rationality and by staying unaware of the fact that the ego is concretely constituted, perceived a conscious ego aware of itself and, by naturalizing it, it also rationalized it. The ego psychology voluntarily--yet maybe innocently--forged deceptions, fashioned fantasies and built a reality that it thought of as "real." The ego that, according to Lacan, prevented one from living an authentic life, the defense against the recognition of the falsity of one's fantasies and the same cause of insanity, became the foundation of a mental fitness. From a precarious champion of fictions the ego became a cherished blessing. What, from Lacan's point of view, could be more tragic?

---

[47]Ibid., p. 173.
[48]Ragland-Sullivan, Ellie, Jacques Lacan and the Philosophy of Psychoanalysis, Chicago: University of Illinois Press, 1987, p. 121.
[49]Lacan, Écrits, p. 169.

3. *Lacan's Critique*

Lacan took a critical stance towards ego psychology. He saw the discrepancies with Freud's theories concerning the dynamic structure of the ego and his insistence on psychogenesis, that is, the psychological mechanisms, and not the organicity of the mental process. Ego psychology missed the ego's fictional, distorting function, the fact that "the ego is structured exactly like a symptom. At the heart of the subject, it is only a privileged symptom, the human symptom *par excellence,* the mental illness of man."[50] For Lacan, there is no separation between conscious and unconscious, two systems that overlap; indeed, he did not separate these realms. The line between conscious and unconscious is not clear, he thought. The ego is not an agent whose defense mechanisms veil unconscious truth and it does not recognize reality as an independent whole, but sees it as a source of immediate gratification or disappointment that provokes strong hostility.[51] In fact, there is no agent at all--the subject is dead, so to say.

Lacan saw the presumptions of ego and behavior psychology as monistic concepts of human personality. For him there are no stable entities (including the self) that exist independently of one's cognitive processes. Applying a self-centered theory and method that is based on an analysis of defenses, the ego psychologists overlook the fact that realities are mainly socially and historically specified and that the subject is socially constituted by knowledge that already exists in the social context, that is, the world of meanings, and affects it through its social interaction. Ego psychology is an impoverished psychology that, by giving a single explanation of human behavior, applies a one-sided overvaluation and denies and ignores the

---

[50]Lacan, Book I, p. 16.
[51]Bychowski, p. 115.

complexity of mental processes. Lacan regarded the theories and methods of ego and behavior psychology as conformist, individualistic, anti-intellectual and he was provoked to return to depth psychology and the investigation of the unconscious and its laws. Because the other views assert that nothing can be in the mind of which one cannot be aware, he considered them as treacherous and as showing impatience with painful complexities.

Ego psychologists claim that their primary criterion is the well-being of the patient and his or her success and happiness in the social matrix, and reinforce a cult of success along with its pretensions. Lacan says in the *Ecrits:*

> The terms of psychoanalytic intervention--the problem of which I am posing here--make it sufficiently clear, I think, that its ethic is not an individualist one. But its practice in the American sphere has been so summarily reduced to a means of obtaining "success" and to a mode of demanding "happiness" that it should be pointed out that this constitutes a repudiation of psychoanalysis, a repudiation that occurs among too many of its adherents from the simple, basic fact, that they have never wished to know anything about the Freudian discovery, and that they will never know anything about it, even by way of repression: for it is a question here of the mechanism of systematic *me-connaissance* in so far as it simulates delusion, even in its group forms.[52]

Ego Psychology and Behaviorism maintain therapies of compromise between emotional forces and the resisting defenses and offer a merely symptomatic relief. Desire persists and the repressed returns

---

[52]Lacan, Écrits, p. 127-8.

sometimes yielding an acting out. Not only do they not attack the pathological cause, but they, in fact, reinforce it, and the process that forces the reality principle on the subject may become an additional traumatic experience:

> One cannot recall without a sense of shame the criteria of success in which this shoddy work culminates: the achievement of a higher income, and the emergency exit provided by the affair with one's secretary, regulating the release of forces strictly bound up in marriage, career and the political community, do not seem to me to be worthy of an appeal... to the Discord of the instincts of life and death.

As Harold A. Sackeim observes, "Were happiness the single measure of psychological health, individuals capable of maintaining pleasure-oriented self-deceits should be viewed as "healthier" than those less happy but more accurate in self-knowledge."[54] The above methods' social retraining becomes a branch of morality, but it is indeed unethical to equate health with "better behavior" and the "true" with adaptation to a preconceived notion of reality. The matrix itself is constantly shifting--since consistency and maintenance of one truth are more related to death rather than life. Then, to what "reality" should one adapt?

They also stress the individual over the social, adaptation over transformation, and the human pursuit of the preservation of life at

---

[53]Ibid., p. 243.

[54]Sackeim Harold A, "Self-Deception, Self-Esteem, and Depression: The Adaptive Value of Lying to Oneself," in Empirical Studies of Psychoanalytical Theories, Vol.1. ed. Joseph Masling, The Analytic Press, 1983, p. 122.

any cost, and as such, their goals are culturally determined. They comply with the existing social realities and their relations of power and authority, designating any differentiation from it as "patholog-ical." Behaviorism, in particular, uses determinate means to change individuals and tends to destroy in the mind of the patient any trace of thinking and willing. Lacan is very suspicious of the "thoughtfulness" of these methods:

> Kindness... would be incapable of curing the evil that it engenders. The analyst who desires the subject's well-being repeats that by which he was formed, and sometimes, even, deformed. The most aberrant education has never had any other motive than the well-being of the subject... reduces the source of symptoms to fear... "Go out there. Now you're a good child".[55]

Elsewhere he adds: "For, in so far as the subject places himself in the register of the ego, everything is indeed dominated by the narcissistic relation. Isn't that what we mean when we say for instance that there is an ineliminable narcissistic dimension in all forms of giving?"[56]

The agent (therapist) who dictates the norm is in full control of the patient and the process. The therapy has success when the patient becomes impotent in thinking, in willing and in acting autonomously. As Bychowski demonstrates it, it can also be dreadful:

> ... We may... assume a severe blockage of the frontal [cerebral] apparatus... perhaps it would then be much more

---

[55]Sackeim, p. 256.
[56]Lacan, Book II, p. 216.

than just another arbitrary extension of concepts if we were to speak of countercathexis of the frontal lobe.... Our assumption should prove its validity in helping us in our understanding of the process of recovery as a result of [electro] shock therapy.... This resulted in consecutive interruption of the blockage: the barrage of countercathexis of the frontal apparatus was broken.... In other words, we may say that the dynamic change produced by shock broke the spell of countercathexis and consequently liberated the normal cathexis of frontal lobes.[57]

The dehumanization of this method of intervention is obvious. The loss of control by the patient is involuntary and the analyst--the expert--has complete control. It is a therapy that does not cure but oppresses, affirming and enforcing society's dominant ethic. It is an immoral ideology of intolerance that paralyzes imagination and accepts the other only as long as one conforms, since difference is offensive. This psychiatric destruction of human differences does not cure but increases social pressure and forces its final solution: collectivization. Lacan saw an imperative to protect personal dignity against this form of "mental abdication"[58] and what might be called "cannibalism":

This conviction extends beyond the individual naivety of the subject who believes in himself, who believes that he is himself--a common enough madness, which isn't complete madness, because it belongs to the order of beliefs.... It isn't therefore simply to this naive belief that they want us to return. It is properly speaking a sociological phenomenon,

---

[57]Bychowski, p. 196.
[58]Lacan, Écrits, p. 306.

which concerns analysis as a technique, or if you prefer, as a ceremony, as a priesthood determined within a certain social context.[59]

4. The Death Instinct

According to Lacan, both Ego Psychology and Behaviorism underestimate or ignore fundamental psychic discontent and the death instinct. What one may desire and get satisfaction from may not be part of what one would, conventionally, call healthy and good, but the form of excesses in *jouissance.* Socrates claimed that evil is an error and that "Nobody desires what is evil," but Freud at one point observed that, "The aim of all life is death (entropy)." He wondered what was the desire that fashioned certain hysterical symptoms for its gratification, why there is something in one that sometimes favors loss, defeat, even death. Along these lines, in *Book II,* Lacan wonders: "Why does the repressed system manifest itself with such insistence... if the nervous system is set to reach a position of equilibrium, why doesn't it attain it?"[60]

According to Lacan, satisfaction, the enemy of desire, becomes addictive, and, as long as repetition turns pleasure into displeasure, the pleasure principle is not opposed to the reality principle: "This is where Freud realizes that something doesn't satisfy the pleasure principle... a compulsion to repeat."[61] There must be something else at work in one's life that neither views one the same way oneself does, nor prefers what is good for oneself. In the hysteric, for example, there

---

[59]Lacan, Book II, p. 12.
[60]Ibid., p. 65.
[61]Ibid., p. 61.

is a split between enjoyment and pleasure and one develops certain symptoms that usually place a strong hindrance to one's life, if not frustrate it. But why would the hysteric desire something other than what is pleasant and agreeable to his or her well-being? Isn't it true that everyone would desire things that make one happy and healthy? Is the subject of the hysteric (one who conceals and at the same time gratifies one's desires through symptoms) a rational one, that is, one that has control over its actions?

There are individuals who respond to the insight they gain during therapy with a negative reaction, by becoming worse, not better, and others who are devastated rather than relieved by any kind of success, as if they do want to hold to their shattering patterns, possibly because these have been the ones shaping their identity so far. In Ecrits, Lacan deduces that, "the key to this mystery (the negative therapeutic reaction), it is said, is in the agency of a primordial masochism—in other words, in a pure manifestation of that death instinct whose enigma Freud propounded for us at the height of his experience."[62]

Freud suspected that the unconscious includes the element of morbidity that totally contradicts the pleasure principle. The hypothesis of a "death drive," the perverse intruder beyond the pleasure principle, inferred the existence of an inherent function that resists the full satisfaction based on the pleasure principle and demands some pain. The pleasure principle constantly fails by stumbling on an inherent demand for ignoring the reality principle, a drive in its interior for some displeasure on something that Lacan will call the *object petit á*, the unattainable, the always missed object. Lacan called this "traumatic," paradoxical enjoyment in displeasure and displeasure in pleasure jouissance and placed it in the *Real. Jouissance* is also

---

[62]Lacan, Écrits, p. 101.

the feeling of self-loss, when one surrenders to and lives one's nothingness. The morbid state is a certain mode of living, one that from now on will define life,[63] although for Lacan one is not driven toward death as entropy[64] but one is driven by "death" in the form of excesses in *jouissance*. Along these lines, ŽiŽek says that, "What we call "culture" is therefore, in its very ontological status, *the reign of the dead over life,* i.e., the form in which the "death drive" assumes positive existence."

Any analysis--as well as an ethics--has to take into serious consideration the fact that there are other forces over against the moral law that direct one to act against one's well-being, such as *jouissance* which is not a matter of the will. The evidenced repetition of traumatic scenes disproves the pleasure principle and, on a certain level, every subject wants his destruction, *whether he wants it or not.* ŽiŽek uses the example of the serial killer whom he defines as the scapegoat embodying sacred violence, the madman who compulsively repeats murderous acts.[66]

---

[63]Lacan, Book II, p. 75. However, this drive is not subversive of reality, for it calls attention to the unconscious mental processes to heighten and intensify awareness and, subsequently, to improve rather than subvert the relations of the individual.

[64]"There is something which is distinct from the pleasure principle and which tends to reduce all animate things to the inanimate--that is how Freud puts it ... Not the death of living things. It's human experience, human interchanges, inter-subjectivity. Something of what he observes in man constrains him to step out of the limits of life." Lacan, Book II, p. 80.

[65]S. ŽiŽek, "Why is *Woman* a Symptom of Man?" in Enjoy Your Symptom: Jacques Lacan in Hollywood and Out, New York: Routledge, 1992, p. 54.

[66]ŽiŽek, "Why is *Woman* a Symptom of Man?" p. 57.

There can be no harmony attained between the pleasure principle and the reality principle. It is for this reason that Lacan was fascinated by courtly love. As Žižek explains,

> The lady is such a paradoxical object which curves the space of desire, i.e., which offers us as the way to attain it only endless detours and ordeals--more precisely the lady is in herself nothing at all, a pure semblance which just materializes the curvature of the space of desire.[67]

After the realization of the significance that obscure desires play in one's baffling acts, "pathology" and the ideals of health had to be redefined. The idea of an antagonism and struggle between life and death, health and sickness, the urge for a sense of continuity and harmony cannot be valid assumptions anymore.

5. The Copernican Revolution

With his statement "the ego is no longer master of its own house," Freud set in motion his Copernican Revolution that challenged the Cartesian status of the subject as the foundation and source of knowledge and the author of its own thought, and resisted the Cartesian catastrophe of the identification of the mind with conscious thinking. Intellectual reason or rational intellect and skeptical consciousness are not the primary agents of the human mind anymore.

Freud's "unacceptable" hypothesis of a disorder in the depths of the mind, of the unconscious motives which are not accessible to conscious intentions and moral sensibilities, inverts the Cartesian

---

[67]Ibid., p. 49.

cogito and reveals the gap between thinking and being: the "I" that one thinks about does not correspond or equal with the "I" that thinks. The "I" is not the subject, which is caught in the structure of alienation and cannot find its being in its thought. Consciousness is only one component of the thinking person and self-awareness always involves discrimination and exclusion. What thinks is not identical with what is being thought and, therefore, consciousness should no longer be mistaken for the center.

Freud subverted the Cartesian subject (the presumed identity of subjectivity and conscious thought) and its assurance of itself. He did violence to subjectivity, to who one is and what one's freedoms and rights are in life. He changed self-images and unsettled identities, which are not given anymore and which will always remain uncertain. One, as a subject without subjectivity or with diverse forms of asserting it, cannot be master over one's being. The subject is not transparent to itself, the ego is not autonomous, and thought-- without being or substance--is permanently cut off from understanding. Only the unconscious thinks. The unconscious implies a radical alterity internal to subjectivity: there is a knowledge that cannot be known, a pleasure that cannot be experienced: "... His discovery (Freud's) is that man isn't entirely in man. Freud isn't a humanist."[68]

The implications of Freud's revolution have been enormous. The unassimilable in Freud disrupts and interrogates all the received conceptions of human reason and knowledge, and challenges many assumptions about human subjectivity common to social sciences, humanities and everyday life. Since the existence of the unconscious makes the subject radically incapable of knowing itself, how can it ever claim to know anything else with absolute certainty? As Lacan is

---

[68]Lacan, Book II, p. 72.

wondering, "We are told that man is the measure of all things. But where is his own measure? Is it to be found in himself?"[69]

Lacan will take the Cartesian *cogito,* the detached, self-owning, self-determined, self-defining, the agoraphobic self,[70] the subject of knowledge and science, and make it the object of psychoanalysis. Like Descartes, Lacan doubted and posed the question of the relation between truth and subject. He, however, conceived consciousness as a secondary phenomenon, and subverted and divided it. He displaced the ego as the central, most solid, fixed, unified, "natural" part of the individual, as the "essence" of identity, along with its capacity to know itself and the world, and turned it into "... a synthesis, a synthesis of functions, a function of synthesis.... It's the latest fetish introduced into the holy of holies of a practice that derives its authority from the superiority of the superiors."[71] Human reason, from being the measure of reality, in the hands of Lacan became a defense.

Lacan emphasized Freud's subversiveness and stressed the neglected and repressed aspects of his work: the radical heterogeneity of the unconscious which is not heard or understood by consciousness, the self's radical ex centricity to itself.[72] The unconscious is where the self manifests itself; in the effects it has in the processes of signification, that is, in all activities. The mind is like an iceberg with only a small part of it above the surface, while the hidden, underwater currents is what moves it. Lacan saw in Freud and his understanding that the primary decisions are unconscious; he saw all the scandalous, threatening and subversive quality of psychoanalysis, and extended it

---

[69]Ibid., p. 68.

[70]J. Hillman, "Man is by Nature a Political Animal," in Speculations After Freud, p. 39.

[71]Lacan, Écrits, p. 131 2.

[72]Ibid., p. 171.

by constructing the foundations of a new conception of subjectivity. He went even further and claimed that, "There where I think, I don't recognize myself, I am not, it is the unconscious; there where I am, it is only too clear that I stray from myself."[73] In the *Ecrits*, he also says: "I think where I am not, therefore I am where I do not think."[74] In the place of the certainty of the subject's being, there is not a res but a void, and where there is thinking, there is no I, no consciousness: "I do not know who I am." The subject that *thinks* is not the same as the one that *is*. For Lacan the subject emerges only at the point of a nonrecognition and all formations of the unconscious have this in common, they are accompanied by a "this is not me," "I was not there." The sub-ject is an underneath, a "sujet-là,"[75] an *hypo-keimenon*, something that lies under the forces that constitute one's being and direct one's thought, action and life. But nothing can contain and fully identify and represent all these forces, which may be even self-contradictory and clash with each other. In this new mode of subjectivity the subject is not the highest creature or the final point of evolution, but "out of joint" and excluded from the "order of things."[76]

Lacan's response to Cartesian Cogito

---

[73]"Je vous ai donné la formule percutante de l' ou je ne pense pas, ou je ne suis pas.... Là où je pense, je ne me reconnais pas, je ne suis pas, c'est l' inconscient. Là où je sius, il est trop clair que je m' égare." J. Lacan, L'Envers de la psychanalyse. Text etablis J. A. Miller, Paris: Seuil, 1991, p. 118.

[74]Lacan, Écrits, p. 166.

[75]Lacan, Livre XVII, p. 53.

[76]S. ŽiŽek, "Introduction: Cogito as a Shibboleth," in Cogito and The Unconscious. ed. Slavo ŽiŽek. Durham and London: Duke University Press, 1998, p. 4.

6. *The Three Registers*

For Lacan, individual subjectivity is dialectically organized in unconscious formations operated by three orders. As in Freud, he viewed the self as an apparatus of different systems and not as a centered unity, and formulated the three registers that construct his topography: the Real, the Symbolic and the Imaginary. They are always tied together and form what Lacan calls the Borromean knot: if one link were to be cut, the whole knot would fall apart.

a. The Real

The Real does not refer to "reality" as one usually understands it, that is, the world of ordinary experience and common sense. It is precisely not "reality" in this sense (which is structured by the Imaginary and the Symbolic) but, rather, it is the raw fact, the unprocessed experience of what is, the experience that is impossible to be inscribed or expressed, the not yet symbolized or imagined. The real is that *site* within the subject known as the unconscious desire and its related fantasies--not the unconscious itself. It is the locus of the Other, that radically other. As such, it designates the existence of the (pre-oedipal sexual) drives whose control and repression form the unconscious, which, thus, is neither primordial nor instinctual.[77]

The most important part of mental action, what creates and processes ideas and makes decisions, is unconscious mental activity, which is not a hidden content and of which one can become aware by inference only. The unconscious is a structure with a subject opposed to the consciousness and the "I," and it refers to all processes of which one is not immediately aware. It is a primary force and activity of which one has no direct awareness or knowledge, though it underlies all physical and mental phenomena. The unconscious is the unthink-

---

[77]Lacan, Écrits, p. 170.

able discourse of that which lacks identity, it is itself a non identity. It is the invisible root of everything, what guides present and future thought and behavior, although it never becomes an object. It is the desiring but inaccessible, ineffable, unspeakable "ground" of things, which is always beyond human comprehension and subjective thought. It is not a submerged consciousness, nor is it defined by way of consciousness. In fact, there are not two different processes or components of thinking, conscious and unconscious, but mainly one primary system, the unconscious.

For Lacan, the subject is not the same thing as the ego but the *subject of the unconscious,* divided and split, and "constituted in its nucleus by a series of alienating identifications."[78] Nor is it the cogito the subject of consciousness, but that of the unconscious, and Lacan pleads for the return to this cogito. As M. Dolar also claims, "... there is not an unconscious outside of cogito."[79] Conscious thought does not lead to truth and the subject is "the true subject of the unconscious.... The Lacanian subject is indeed structured as 'cogito.'"[80]

The Real, thus, cannot be experienced as such, nor can it be represented or conceptualized. It is the unstructured, the unimaginable, inarticulate, what is unassimilable in representation, the "impossible" itself. Always remaining out of grasp and being beyond full assimilation into discourse, the Real, the thing in itself, is only indirectly--negatively and inferentially--known. It is the paradoxical memory of what has always been forgotten, the repressed part, the excluded thought that comes always to haunt and dislocate the subject.

But, what is forgotten is recalled in acts,[81] setting a severe peril to

---

[78]Écrits, p. 128.

[79]M. Dolar, "Cogito as the Subject of the Unconscious," in Cogito and the Unconscious, p. 14.

[80]Dolar, p. 21.

[81]Lacan, Écrits, p. 52.

the self, for it threatens to dissolve its Imaginary identity. The Real returns either as aggression or as sublimation. Its language, the expression of the unconscious, is the symptom, the signifier which speaks through the subject--not as the subject--and points to the things one does without knowing it: "It's just that the symptom reappears like weeds."[82] The symptoms, the compromises which try to cure the condition from which they originate, are structured as metaphors, not concealing but indicating the existence of something else.

The unconscious consists of structural laws like grammar, laws that also regulate the unconscious activities. Along with its representations, it is structured like a language, that is, the contents of the unconscious function as signifiers, expressing themselves in terms of metaphors and metonymies (Freud's condensation and displacement). This implies that, if one knew more about the nature and development of language, one would also know the self. The difficulty lies in the contradiction between what is being said and what is being signaled by saying it, precisely because every word has a navel, a blind spot that reaches down into the unknown. Language is always split and inadequate since the Real constantly intervenes. It is precisely this conflict that marks human subjectivity. As language is broken and can infinitely communicate different possibilities of available meanings, in the same way there is an impossibility in integrating the lost part of the unconscious.

Since the unconscious is the discourse of the Other and cannot be articulated in its own voice, it breaks into consciousness and the unspoken speaks through its discourses:

> We always come back, then, to our double reference to speech and to language. In order to free the subject's speech, we introduce him into the language of his desire,

---

[82]Ibid., p. 260.

that is to say, into the *primary language* in which, beyond what he tells us of himself, he is already talking to us unknown to himself, and, in the first place, in the symbols of the symptom.[83]

There is a discrepancy between what is intended to be said and what is actually said and the importance of the phenomena, like verbal slips, is that they testify to the existence of the unconscious. In this gap lies one's desire which makes itself known only by disrupting the customary processes of meaning formation and by subverting the intentions of conscious speech as interruption, silencing, parapraxes, slips of the tongue, eruption, discontinuity, ambiguity, error, psycho-somatic reactions, where the truth of the unconscious resides. The unconscious speaks and desire articulates itself in metonymies and metaphors. Through the unconscious--which consists of signifiers that have been repressed--language speaks the subject and, thus, the conscious discourse is infiltrated by the discourse of the Other. The subject is not the agent of speech, it is no longer the master of language but, rather, language itself constitutes it as such. The vehicle of speech is not the ego, but the "I," the *je.* The subject, this empty form, is not the cause of discourse but the effect of it. The "I think" turns into the "it speaks." The unconscious "happens" on someone and one suffers its pathos.

Precisely because we speak with language and language "speaks" us, we are caught in it and, therefore, we need to speak of language. Lacan was interested in the figures of speech and he indicated the dependence on and the importance of the signifiers and, thus, turned Freud's neurological and psychological model into a linguistic one. Since the unconscious does not consist of instincts but of signifiers and its discourse is governed by signifying mechanisms, and since

---

[83]Écrits, p. 81.

psychoanalysis has only a single medium, the patient's speech,[84] the object of psychoanalysis is discourse and the only techniques of interpretation can be linguistic or literary. Lacan used linguistics, the exploration of the structures discernible in human language, as the paradigm of analysis. He maintained that what he was trying to articulate was that what dominates society is the practice of language.[85]

For Lacan, psychoanalysis is founded on the distinction between signified and signifier, the two components of the sign and the smallest unit of analysis. The signifier and the signified do not constitute two different ontological orders, but two orders of discourse. Both are to be understood psychically, for they are situated within the realm of thought. The signifier is that element of the sign that is not the signified. In *Ecrits*, Lacan gave a definition:

> My definition of a signifier (there is no other) is as follows: a signifier is that which represents the subject for another signifier. This signifier will therefore be the signifier for which all the other signifiers represent the subject: that is to say, in the absence of this signifier, all the other signifiers represent nothing, since nothing is represented only *for* something else.[86]

The subject is itself a sign, the *je* is a cultural signifier. In the *Four Fundamental Concepts of Psychoanalysis,* he also says: "The signifier, producing itself in the field of the other, makes manifest the subject of

---

[84]Ibid., p. 40.

[85]"Ce que j' essaie d' articuler, parce que l' analyse m' en donne le témoignage, c' est ce qui la domine, à savoir la pratique du langage." Lacan, Livre XVII, p. 239.

[86]Lacan, Écrits, p. 316.

its signification. But it functions as a signifier only to reduce the subject in question to being no more than a signifier, to petrify the subject in the same movement in which it calls the subject to function, to speak, as subject."[87]

Lacan followed Saussure who opposed the tendency to regard language as a "naming process only, as a list of words, each corresponding to the thing that it names."[88] For him, speech is the execution of language that is a (social) system of signs. However, unlike Saussure, he favored the signifier, that is, the material element in the genesis of a concept (the signified), because the signified is simply another signifier: "no significations can be sustained other than by reference to another signification: in its extreme form, this amounts to the proposition that there is no language in existence for which there is any question of its inability to cover the whole field of the signified."[89]

Because of the arbitrariness of the relationship between signified and signifier, the signified is occasioned by the relations between the signifiers. A particular signifier refers to a signified only through the mediation of the whole chain of signifiers that continually slides over the chain of signifieds. Lacan analogized the chain of signifieds with the contextual, circumstantial arrangements of signifiers. The correspondence of a particular signifier to a particular signified can only occur in a particular context. As a letter of the alphabet has no meaning by itself but a fundamental function in the creation of words and sentences that carry meaning, the meaning that determines the unconscious destiny of the subject depends on the way the signifiers

[87]J. Lacan, <u>Four Fundamental Concepts of Psychoanalysis</u>, ed. Jacques-Alain Miller, trans. Alan Sheridan, New York: Norton, 1978, p. 207.

[88]F. De Saussure, <u>Course in General Linguistics</u>, ed. C. Bally and A. Riedlinger, trans. W. Baskin, New York: McGraw-Hill, 1966, p. 65.

[89]Lacan, <u>Écrits</u>, p. 150.

are organized and related among each other, on the mechanism of their combination. And as with letters, meaning is also the product of the way other meanings are structured and organized. Todd May adds that, "In order for meaning to occur, identity must exist within difference, or better, each must exist each within the other. To speak with Saussure, if language is a system of differences, it is not only difference but system as well; and system carries within it the thought of identity. Putting the matter baldly, a thought of pure difference is not a thought at all."[90]

The signifiers do not "express" the reality of things. They *are* this reality, all that one can have. Since thought depends on the signifiers, things as well as ideas are products of language formulations. Language, thus, has ontological significance, forming and governing reality: "For it is still not enough to say that the concept is the thing itself... it is the world of words that creates the world of things."[91] In the same way, cognition depends upon interactions that rest on changing patterns of relation. It is also knowledge that is constituted by the signifiers that formulate it. When the signifiers alter their arrangement, knowledge is also modified or replaced. In this way, the various areas of sciences and arts, not only give a better understanding of the world, but also, by building symbolic systems as the ideal points of reference, they create new worlds of which one had no awareness before. They did not exist in any manner at the level of our perception.[92] In the same manner, the signifiers, the mutually differentiated signs, can also regulate psychological development. Changes in discourse create changes in social and psychological realities, and experience is

---

[90]T. May, "From Ontological Difference to Ontological Holism: Gilles Deleuze," in Reconsidering Difference, The Pennsylvania State University Press, 1997, p. 193.

[91]Lacan, Écrits, p. 65.

conditioned by linguistic effects, in fact, subjectivity is an effect, an embodiment of relations. The existence of the subject itself depends on the world of signifiers, that is, the essential disparity of signification and being; one can only remain a subject by holding on to the signifiers.

The fact that no single signifier is definitely attached to a single signified reveals a constitutive *lack* of any fixed meaning. And since there is no absolute foundation of meaning--because the Other has no unity and, therefore, no center--meaning is always in a "signifying movement," never fixed, permanent or intelligible. A signifier will always stay free to make new connections and meanings. Having no meaning in themselves but only a potential one, signifiers stay essentially open and ambiguous. With linguistics language faces its own liminality, its limitations, and, paradoxically, also its endless potentialities.

b. The Imaginary

The Imaginary is the register of psychic life dominated by relations to images of one's self and others. As the world of fantasy, it is a peculiar mode of existence and experience associated with closed dyadic relations, identifications, fixations and narcissism.

It is in the mirror stage where the imaginary dimension of one's life originates, and which is carried forward into all later development as a fundamentally narcissistic fascination that tends to draw all relationships into an unrealistic and futile striving for identification with the ideal "other," whether this is one's own image, the mother, or another object (the *petit á*).

---

[92]Lacan, Livre XVII, p. 184. Lacan very often mentions the oracle in *Oedipus* as the signifier that determined the hero's life: "... signifiers determine our fate as mortals ... determine our existence."

According to Lacan, there is an inescapable and fatal fact: The human infant, in comparison with animals, is born prematurely. This biological, organic insufficiency, forces the child, which has no awareness of its corporeal boundaries and cannot distinguish between itself and its environment, to depend on others for its survival. The child, which is born into the order of the Real not as an integrated psychical or corporeal unity, but as a series of organs, parts, impulses and needs, confronts a fundamental lack, *manque á étre,* the lack of being. Yet, the infant also wants-to-be: "the radical and humanly unsatisfiable yearning of the infant for the lost paradise of complete fusion with its All--a wanting born of want."[93]

The child's first recognition of lack or absence of the mother and the gratification of its needs is the moment around which the mirror stage revolves--sometime between the age of 6 and 18 months. The acknowledgment of this lack or loss induces it into identificatory relations and the child enters an imaginary relation with the other who can be the mothering person who serves as model of a wholeness, or with its own reflected image through which the child experiences itself as a whole and as a unity and becomes capable of distinguishing itself from the outside world. The infant, therefore, misidentifies with its own reflection as well as with the images of others, including external things, and this identification gives it the illusion of totality and being. As Lacan says in *Écrits,* "What I have called paranoiac knowledge is shown, therefore, to correspond in its more or less archaic forms to certain critical moments that mark the history of man's mental genesis, each representing a stage in objectifying identification."[94]

From now on, lack and loss will be the mode of being and the

---

[93]J. P. Muller and W. J. Richardson, Lacan and Language: A Reader's Guide to Écrits, New York: International University Press Inc., 1982, p. 22.

subject will always attempt to fill it. Any mental phenomenon will not be a psychical event that can be differentiated from the subject, but an imago, a group of unconscious representations. The mirror stage becomes the foundation for all the subsequent errors that will entrap it, for all the méconnaissance, those refusals to recognize reality-- ironically, the same refusals that constitute the ego. This misrecognition is persistent because it is gratifying; through it one achieves a sense of being since it seems to promise unity, completeness and autonomy of the self.

According to Lacanian psychoanalysis, psychosis is a desperate effort to hold on to such a delusion originating in an ambiguity between presence and absence. Its manifestation is the failure to sustain boundaries as in the case of the failure to admit and suffer absence or to differentiate the image from the object. In psychosis, when the object of desire is not there, it is not simply imagined but *believed* to be there. What makes this "presence" a certainty is not a profane quality but a faith,[95] the imagining of the presence of something absent, a delusion--and this is what makes any belief suspect.

The child, thus, identifies with an image of itself that is always also an image of another. The "I" indeed is an other. The subject is always elsewhere than where it is, because it can see and know itself only in an image of itself. The infant's "self" is not innate but constructed on a false recognition of the other as the same. This reflected, imaginary, and alien

---

[94]Lacan, Écrits, p.17.

[95]As Ferenczi states it, a woman is a stranger to her own non-phantasy and non-imaginary feminine body experience because she is lost in her phantasy. If her phantasy of having a penis becomes sufficiently "real," she will imagine not that she has a penis, but that she has *not* got one. Imagination is then used to imagine what one has not got in phantasy. In Laing, Self and Other, p. 44.

image generates the ego that begins to be constituted and to take shape. The ego is this internalization of otherness, the imaginary *moi*, the same agent of *méconnaissance*, and its genesis is a defense, since this ego-image is not a self-realization but a self-idealization. It is not centered on the perception-consciousness system or the reality principle, but it is characterized by the function of miscognition and denial.

The center of the self is the unconscious, that is, desire, the fundamental driving force that originates in this rupture of the union with the mother. From now on, it will relate to her through desire, trying to get her recognition. The Imaginary is the tragic register which accommodates the irreparable loss of the (m)other, a wound that will never be healed. At the heart of this negation for deliverance is the desire to restore the shattered unity, to find the lost object that, in fact, one never had. Later in life, madness will be disguised as love and the lover will seek and demand in the beloved what he or she lacks, as if the other possesses a fullness that will complete the subject. Yet, there is nothing for them to exchange besides their lack, the endless dynamism of desires.

One mimics the image one identifies with until one unreflectively reflects it, or projects it on someone else--as on the analyst--or sees oneself from a distance, reflectively. In the process of identification, which is motivated by one's egoism while it also reinforces it, the individual not only loses a clear sense of difference from the other, but also confuses one's and the other's desires. The mirror stage and its fantasies is the ground on which the subject will narcissistically form not only its ideal egos but also its ego-ideals and will identify with and achieve identity by imitating what the other imitates. The child--who desires what its mother desires--does not simply copy appearances but also tendencies, modes, and values. The subject also seeks to master the other's desire and sees itself as the object of the other's desire and, by imaginative identification, also seeks to desire him/ herself with that same desire. Desire is the "desire of the Other,"[96] that is, the desired object of the (m)other.

As it was argued earlier, the lack in being makes being fundamentally defective. One identifies with persons, images, and so forth because one lacks innate being and wants to eradicate this loss by bridging the void within and without. The ego is formed from the outside world, an imaginary constellation of identifications, added and subtracted throughout life. One desires what the others desire, and satisfaction is also pursued by way of others: desiring wholeness, two persons try to fill each other's lacks: "The subject doesn't have a dual relation with an object with which he is confronted, it is in relation to another subject that his relations with this object acquire their meaning, and... their value."[97] Depending on one another for its "self," the subject is always already implicated in the other that has a fundamental primacy in the formation of subjectivity.

The ego, therefore, is not centered on a system of perception consciousness, since perception is imaginary and not an innate system, but it exists in the site of the illusions of imagination. It is rather structured by the function of *méconnaissance,* which, however, is not recognized as such. This misrecognition of the truth of the fragmentation, helplessness, lack, of the nothingness of the self, this fantasy, is what constitutes identity: "I have illusions, therefore I am." The dimension of fantasy is constitutive of the subject--there is no subject without fantasy: "I fantasize therefore I am."[98] Lacan thought that the theory of the subject must be reformulated along the lines of fantasy. Selfhood can be defined only in terms of an imaginary self, a lack, an absence lying at the heart of the ego. The self is always an invention of the imagination, the empty space in which fantasies are projected, a texture without substance, a temperament without

---

[96]Lacan, Écrits, p. 264.

[97]Lacan, Book II, p. 255.

[98]"... dreams that are going on "in broad daylight," Lacan, Écrits, p. 261.

constitution. There is no structure of centralized control and the self's truth is always already alienated. One's mind is rather a bricolage of multiple agents who collaborate bottom-up and whose organization is shifting, adaptable and occasional.

The process of identification at the mirror stage, the procedure by which a human being comes to exist as such by identifying with his or her semblance, constitutes a fundamental and fatal error. It will be repeated throughout life in relation to the images of other people that will define him or her ontologically and psychologically. The subject is not that object or any other, but what it would like to be, and its pursuit of a state as the ideal object becomes the driving force of its life. Evoking one's presence in the place of one's absence, one will design ideal egos *(moi)* based on ego-ideals (others), a division that indeed defines the ego as split. Part of the self is experienced in others. The other will become the core of the self and it will give to the individual its "social" identity. The image will be *and* will be not an image of itself.

Systematically misrecognizing reality, the ego will always be subverted from within by its own tendency to identification with the objects it encounters in the course of life. Identity will always be constituted through the mediation of others, and individual being and life will be determined by the actions that are conditioned by the way the elements of the specific environment are internalized:

> ... the unconscious is the discourse of the other... not the discourse of the abstract other... it is the discourse of the circuit in which I am integrated. I am one of its links. It is the discourse of my father for instance, in so far as my father made mistakes which I am absolutely condemned to reproduce... because I am obliged to pick up again the discourse he bequeathed to me... because one can't stop the chain of discourse, and it is precisely my duty to transmit it in its aberrant form to someone else.... That's

what the need for repetition is, as we see it emerge beyond the pleasure principle... it is only introduced by the register of language.[99]

In this projective identification, one will cling to external formulas and "live" by living through the lives of others. But sooner or later, one will sense in one's actions a lack of intrinsic meaning. On this Roudinesco comments: "In so doing he [Lacan] made all human freedom dependent on a temporal event: to each individual comes a *"temps pour comprendre"* (time for comprehending) in the light of which he can make a logical decision.... One cannot foresee how long it will take one to understand....."[100]

Because there is always a movement toward identification with the specular image projected into or onto the other, every such relation is threatened with absorption into narcissism. As Lacan says in *Book II,* "... if we look at out neighbor and think that he's thinking what we're thinking, it's a gross error."[101] Narcissism here refers to the ego constituting itself by identification with an image, the looking at oneself through the other and one's love for oneself via the other, the ego-ideal: "... in any narcissistic relation, the ego is the other, and the other is me *[moi]*."[102] The narcissistic self sees the other as the extension of itself. In one's love of one's neighbor one loves the image by which his or her ego was formed; one flees differences from others and loves what reflects one's self.

---

[99]Lacan, Book II, p. 89-90.

[100]Elizabeth Roudinesco, Jacques Lacan, trans. Barbara Bray. New York: Columbia University Press, 1997, p. 178, 194.

[101]Lacan, Book II, p. 188.

[102]Ibid., p. 96.

Yet, there is a dual, ambivalent relation to this image of identification, a divided attitude that can have no final resolution. What causes a mad or a criminal act has its roots in the imaginary identifications. Since the ego only comes into being by identifying with something outside the person, as the foundation and support of one's identity and at the same time what annihilates it, its autonomy could only come from the suppression of the very image upon which its existence depends. There is a conflict between the desire to melt and the desire to set free, and an inherent aggressivity is directed to one's self-image because one strives to deny its dependence on others. The power one has on someone else creates fear for him or her, and bases the fundamental desire one has to hurt others. What the criminal kills is something deep about him/her, his/her tie to the other. As Gilbert Chaitin observes, by itself "the dependence on otherness would not be so damaging; it is the fact that the ego is formed through the denial of that very process of alienation which may lead to... disastrous results."[103] Jane Gallop agrees: "Somehow the avoidance of tragedy depends upon a retroactive... acceptance of one's foundations (whether concepts of self) as fiction."[104] And, as Mark Taylor also observes, "If the subject does not need to repress the other "within," it is not driven to oppress the other "without."[105]

Lacan concluded that the ego is solely a narcissistic, pathological construct and this is rooted in the history of the imaginary: "This ego, whose strength our theorists now define by its capacity to bear frustration, is frustration in its essence."[106] What paranoids seek to do is to mend the split between the real and the ideal, between who they are and who they want to be.

---

[103]G.D. Chaitin, "Lacan's Return to Freud," Salmagundi, 106/107, Spring/Summer 1995, p. 307-8.

[104]J. Gallop, Reading Lacan., Ithaca: Cornell University Press, 1985, p. 90.

[105]M. C. Taylor, Erring: A Postmodern A/theology, p. 147.

[106]Lacan, Écrits, p. 42.

Lacan based his theory of the three registers on this view of human nature. He, thus, reconceptualized the foundations of psychoanalysis on a tragic basis and claimed ignorance of the self, which is not a stable, recognizable entity, but a fusion of inside and outside, a collage, a collection of partial views juxtaposed in such a way that there is no single view, no unique perspective. Recognizing that there is no consistency that can contain all truth, Lacan did not attempt to resolve the contradictions and conflicts that he saw inherent in life, and in his work he constantly failed to bring deliverance and resolution. He saw suffering as founded on the fundamental lack and insufficiency of human nature, on the internal and integral inadequacy. For this reason Lacan's psychoanalysis is tragic.

This misrecognition and ontological incompleteness sets profound epistemological obstacles. The subject also misrecognizes external things. Lacan saw the limits of a self-sufficient reason, and focused on the power of deception and on one's systematic misrecognition of reality, on the lack of any distinct border between reality and illusion, true and false. For him, human knowledge, caught in fantasy, betrays a profound ignorance, and certainty and objectivity are impossible. In *Some Reflections on the Ego,* Lacan says that, "... we are led to see our objects as identifiable egos, having unity, permanence, and substantiality; this implies an element of inertia, so that the recognition of objects and of the ego itself must be subjected to constant revision in an endless dialectical process."[107] In the unpublished notes by Francoise Dolto, Lacan is quoted to say that "Man does not adapt himself to reality; he adapts reality to himself."[108]

---

[107]J. Lacan, "Some reflections on the Ego: 1951," International Journal of Psychoanalysis, 34:11-17 (1953): 12.

Reality, as something not external and given, but as constituted by the subject, is thus a fiction. There is always a black stain in its very heart. Žižek also states that, "The very idea of the universe, of all of reality, as a totality that exists in itself, is thus rejected as a paralogism: what appears as an *epistemological limitation* of our capacity to grasp reality (the fact that we are forever perceiving reality from our finite, temporal standpoint), is the positive *ontological condition* of reality itself."[109]

The fictitiousness of reality, however, does not make it innocent and harmless. The mirror stage also grounds the symbolic functions that will organize all the subject's relations with the world, organizing its associations with others, its perspective, how it would orient itself in the world, its entire reality. From this arbitrary perspective, the subject will look at itself and pass ethical judgments. These fictions have real effects: they dominate and regulate one's actual lives and self-experience; they make treaties or declare wars. What is true of persons applies also to international relations. The entire ethical, political, legal, religious and other orders that regulate a community and establish its values are constituted by similar nonentities; something that does not exist takes the form of our lives.

The claim, hence, that the subject is divided does not mean that it does not exist, that it is a nothing.[110] As M. Dolar says, "Nothing remains, but this nothing counts."

HUMAN RELATIONS

Roudinesco comments on Lacan's aspiration to attract Catholics who opposed any biological reading and materialistic aspect of Freud,

---

[108]F. Dolto, *Unpublished Notes.* (June 16, 1936), in Roudinesco, Jacques Lacan, p. 114.

[109]Žižek, "Introduction: Cogito as a Shibboleth," p. 5.

[110]Alcorn, "The subject of Discourse," p. 27.

a Freud who claimed the development of one's personality as independent from biological facts, such as instinct, race and heredity, a view that would have various implications for the notion of individuality and particularity. Although Lacan did not deny the role that the individual biological structure and organic causality may play in the formation of one's personality and one's decisions in the course of life altogether, he rejected any fundamental dependence on it. Language, for example, exists before one is born and it conditions any biological development.

Lacan also rejected any understanding of human nature based on constitutionalism, the belief that there is an essence that constitutes human personality and, therefore, a static entity functioning. He evaluated human personality in a Freudian, yet philosophical way, and developed a new notion of selfhood. The way one is in the world is primarily made up by the individual and his or her own environment. In Lacan's thought there is a fundamental primacy of structure. Three factors determined what Lacan implied by *personality: biographical development,* that is, the "facts" in one's life and the way they have been experienced; *self-concept,* referring to the way one perceives oneself; and *tension of social relations* referring to the impact one thinks that has on others.[112] By invalidating the doctrine of constitutions, he gave to human relationships a new meaning and importance.

The individual is seen in terms of his or her social existence made up of a complex web of different kinds of inclinations, preferences, roles, and behaviors. The subject is the empty point of self-relating, and it is modified by the processes in which it partakes. As Foucault would also say, subjective experience is not private but public, and,

---

[111]Dolar, "Cogito as the Subject of the Unconscious," p. 16.
[112]Roudinesco, p. 45.

since the subject is historically constituted by and defined as identifications, it does not coincide with the individual. The entire personality, which interacts with a social milieu, is the product of social activity. The self emerges from social interaction, identities are intermingled in a net of intersubjectivity, and self-identity is actualized only within a network of conditioning mutual relationships. What gives one an identity is one's relationships with others, and the mere presence of another person can be very powerful and influential. Every subject and its roles are determined by one's belonging and integration to the symbolic order of mutual relationships in which one person complements the identity of the other. What defines a father as such is his child, a wife is her husband: identity requires an other. The symbolic law assigns to everyone a role and a place, and one submits to a forced destiny.

The subject is, thus, the sum of enacted conscious and unconscious representations that confront society in general, and they either coincide with or are opposed to the ways others view it. To have an identity in such a web may be really trapping. One may acquire a concrete role--which one does not relish--simply because one is associated with particular individuals. One may agree with Laing who says that,

> a person's "own" identity cannot be completely abstracted from his identity-for-others. His identity-for-himself; the identity others ascribe to him; the identities he attributes to them; the identity or identities he thinks they attribute to him; what he thinks they think he thinks they think.... Other people become a sort of identity kit, whereby one can piece together a picture of *oneself.*

One of the definitions of madness has been the state in which one's view of oneself does not correspond with the way the others describe him or her and who falls a victim of the fictions of others. But "It is difficult not to accept their story.... We learn to be whom we are told we are."[113]

Although it is painful to recognize the discrepancy between how one sees oneself and how one is seen by others, this confining definition of identity can be also liberating, since one can choose one's personal relations or the testimony one gives about his or her self: "One's self-identity is the story one tells one's self of who one is."[114] And, since in one social setting there may exist more than one discourse systems, one can change the network by relocating at different discourse systems and re-defining one's identity which remains variable, inconsistent and confused. Lacan viewed some paranoids as "awkward squads" who are not willing or able to conform to the social contexts in which they find themselves: "If he is lucky and fate puts him in the right place, he may become a social or cultural reformer, a 'great intellectual."[115]

Many forces pull one apart in different directions and diverse and contradictory identifications make for diversified identities, and each one is a particular effect, while some may be more complicated or mystified than others. Nor is one the same in every situation, in crowds or behind closed doors. "Multi-personality disorder" is everyone's condition. As one can accommodate more than one social and private identities, there may be no such thing as "mistaken identity", although there will always be the feeling of not real "me". Everyone is "disordered" and "multiple personality" is normal.

---

[113] Ronald D. Laing, Self and Others, Tavistock, 1969, p. 78.

[114] Ibid., p. 76.

[115] Roudinesco, p. 24-25. Roudinesco comments on Lacan's own "Bovary-like desire for a change of identity" and she claims that he would have had a different one "... if instead of pursuing a career in medicine he had lapsed into wandering and delusion." p. 47.

Although Lacan's radical intersubjectivity attacks individualism and his psychoanalysis is not isolated from societal systems, it preserves particularity. Still, however, the focus is on the individual as a whole. The observation that many subjects are born and raised in the same context but no two of them are identical compels one to think that, although a subject may reflect a social system, it is not equivalent to it. External circumstances are the occasion but not the causes. Although both environment and biology and organic determinants are the causes as well as the effects of one's structure and behavior, there must be some other levels of organization within the subject that also operate and determine the way the same signifying mechanisms affect in different ways and determine different "destinies". Lacan suggests a multiplicity of factors: history, tradition, and heredity, what is beyond the control of any individual, some other "animalistic" forces, and chance. Yet, there is an optimism in Lacan, a belief--his only belief--in human imagination and creativity. External circumstances are occasions but not causes, since the subject is not restricted in adopting and reflecting existing structures passively. Lacan left space for personal choice and he held that the individual has some leverage on the context in which it finds itself, some space for creativity and transformation, since ambiguity involves openness to various possibilities. The creative power of the human psyche is irreducible; no one ever stops fantasizing. As Cornelius Castoriadis also insists, there is a creative and radical imagination in both the human psyche and the imaginary institution of society that can never be exhaustively explained away by any system of thought outside it.[116]

Since both individuals and communities build systems of fantasies,

---

[116]Cornelius Castoriadis, "Psychoanalysis and Politics," in Speculations After Freud, p. 5.

one needs to assess which of these pseudo-realities are the most valid and "healthy". But, since every reality is a meconnaissance, a mis-recognition, and since, according to Lacan, we all rest our lives on pseudo-realities, it is like asking to judge which one is less of a meconnaissance, and, therefore, the problem of quality becomes an issue of degree: Which reality is more real and what are the degrees of fantasy? How far should one stretch the boundaries that determine what fantasies are acceptable, in what contexts and when, and why would one want to trespass them? How do these systems impose themselves? The answers to these questions create vicious circularities.

As long as one "lives in" a fantasy and is immersed in it, one can recognize it as such only in retrospect, when one has already emerged from it. This may imply the complete immersion in another one, which means that the assessment of value and degree has already been made.[117] Is there any chance to get out from all fantasies and live in a "real" reality? In The Seminar of J. Lacan: Book II: The Ego, Lacan says: "If the symbolic function functions, we are inside it. And I would even say--we are so far into it that we can't get out of it."[118] Ronald David Laing agrees: "The more untenable a position is, the more difficult it is to get out of it.... By untenable, I mean that it is impossible to leave and impossible to stay."[119] And as he also says later, when one is in such a situation, one does not realize this and, thus, it is impossible to get out.

As has already been said, "stepping out of" may be perceived as madness. If one wants to step beyond the shared phantasy system and what society maintains as real, one will be classified as "mad," not

---

[117]"... the problem lies not in the reality that is lost, but in that which takes its place." Lacan, Écrits, p. 189.

[118]Lacan, Book II, p. 31.

[119]Laing, Self and Others, p. 26.

without justification, since madness, as a rescuer from the unbearable conflicts, is a way out.

Generally, people living their ordinary lives do not reflect on the social fantasy systems, which are been taken for granted. Even if they do, they may decide not to engage themselves in a struggle for freedom, which, in fact, will always be frustrated by the unconscious determinations. Their self and world are the "real" ones, because they either cannot or are unwilling to notice their symptoms as such and the desire that they envelop. This ignorance may be the result of a comfortable and rewarding lot, one that lacks any violence that would force one to think. Or it may be the consequence of an ardent devotion to the social fantasies in a desperate attempt for acceptance and approval, something that makes the relevance of environment to the origins of schizophrenia apparent and indisputable, for, consensus with a shared phantasy system does not exclude the existence of conflict. One may wonder, who is in a more favorable position, the one who is not aware of any rupture, or the one who lives a reflected life and discerns conflicts? The one who knows that his or her whole life is a complicated symptom that masks desire, or the one who is inno-cently ignorant?

For Lacan humans are not free. The self is not autonomous and its decisions are not entirely its own, so it is not entirely responsible. Yet, personal decisions share in the responsibility for the different ways one filters and contains the social knowledge one receives as well as his or her experiences, and how, consequently, one chooses the way one orients oneself in the world. The subject is not restricted in adopting and reflecting existing structures passively. It has also the capacity to produce original discourses that will constitute itself and, potentially, others or a society at large who will adopt it. One owns the precious gift to be capable in changing orientations and turn to discourses yet unstructured or unknown. By responding and processing knowledge in different ways, by taking different positions in relation to discourse, one develops particular conflicts, and, as a consequence, different and original discourses that both reflect and try to resolve them. In other words, these different conflicts are the evidences of the radical heterogeneity of the other.[120]

Since the "self" and the world are not only social or psychological or linguistic--aspects that can be manipulated--but also structural, everyone does indeed perceive the world in a different way. It is not a matter of different perspectives but of different organizations and positions: neither are we all the same nor are we always facing the same direction.

c. The Symbolic

The dual imaginary relations need to be symbolically regulated. What makes this transition possible is the involvement of a third notion, the "symbolic" order. The Other is embodied in the figure of the symbolic father who enters the dual imaginary and narcissistic structure of identifications and gratifications. The Symbolic is the realm of signification, of making sense, and the realm of cause and effect. Lacan calls it the *"Other",* the law of symbolic functioning, the paternal metaphor, because it is associated with the realm of social and cultural symbolism and laws, of differentiation and pluralistic relations, of language, of anything that is specifically human, of all that constitutes the actual human world in which one finally has to find a way to live as a mature, responsible person.[121] It is needed as a means of restricting the inexorable human aggressiveness and for ensuring the society's long-term preservation. Yet, the Law is not only the

---

[120]Alcorn, "The Subject of Discourse," p. 41.

[121]E. Webb, "The New Social Psychology of France: The Heritage of Jacques Lacan," Religion 23, Jan 1993: 61-69.

[122]Lacan calls it the 'Law of the Father' because the fathers usually make the laws (Although he refers more to the dead father of Freud's Totem and Taboo), and also because of its necessity and universality.

negative law of prohibitions, but it has a positive and productive dimension as well.[122]

The Other is a massive system of patterns and relationships (myths, immediate family, ethnic background etc.) that is other than what the subject is conscious of. It is the symbolic function that lies behind whatever is "natural", given, precisely because it is the law that governs the unconscious organization of human societies. These unconscious principles that organize the contexts are in fact what make one a subject. As products and safeguards of a setting, these non-natural values, socially patterned, internalized and embodied repetitions, will organize one's fragments, perception, language, thought and action, and formulate one's self-image, identity and personal history and life. One becomes an image, a representation of one's models, the reflection of his or her particular social discourse. In this way, as J. Hillman also claims, the self is the interiorization of community.[123]

Since the symbolic, the Other, is the dimension beyond individual subjects, it is constructed through difference. It emphasizes the importance and preference of the other over the self and, thus, it is the social space in which community can take place: "The only ground of identity, of meaning, of representation, is in fact the non ground of the play of difference, the "symbolic"... the aspect of human subjectivity which tends to escape from this realm of objectification by means of differentiation."[124]

In this way Lacan redefined the subject within its community. Humans are "social animals" structured and governed by symbolic orders whose identifications grant them a place in the intersubjective space which, in its turn, consists of a clutter of detached fragments and

---

[123]Hillman, "Man is by Nature a Political Animal," p. 35.
[124]Chaitin, "Lacan's Return to Freud," p. 8.

processes of functions which can be endlessly rearranged under different conditions, since the Other is not necessarily consistent. The often irregular Law structures the way identity and desire happen in one's life, as well as morality, what it permits or prohibits. Only, these embodied fragments and processes are the effect of external, social forces that do not act directly but mediate through unconscious structures and forces that have already been determined before the birth of the subject. As the result of the context in which one lives his or her early years and the effect of its discourse, one is affected by particular characteristics, habits, values, ideals and knowledge that develop certain patterns that will become and stay dominant in later life. The individual internalizes, that is, accepts fully, the existing institutions of society, the imaginary significations which organize a community and which give meaning to the individual and his or her life.[125] The social milieu has a determining influence on the structuration of the unconscious that is structured like the language of the specific social matrix. Thought itself is composed of interlinked signifying chains that in turn are made up by the functions of the three orders. One does not think from one's "mind", a preordained place that holds knowledge. The tremendous force the social knowledge has--which affects the subject through social interactions--will eventually create a "fixation", a blocking force that will be the main basis for resistance in the process of analysis. Even when the fragments and functions get modified, they will do so according to certain enduring patterns.

Yet, it is not only individuals who do not realize that the content of their experience is a fantasy. Since there are developments of psychic mechanisms within the family and society, there are psychotic families and cultures as well. Whole communities are constructed, organized

---

[125]Castoriadis, "Psychoanalysis and Politics," p. 6.
[126]Lacan, Book II, p. 49.

and held together by inner identifications that create their pseudo-realities and become the essence of their social bonds: "There are illusions that are perfectly objective."[126] While the members of groups identify with one another, the existence of groups themselves presupposes an organization around an identification with an object (the father, the leader, God, ideas and so forth) that replaces their own particular ego-ideals. Whole cultures function in similar ways. With the power of indirect suggestions, individuals are made to deny the particular ways they experience the world, and develop and establish social fantasy systems that reflect and determine the community's values, categories and course in history. In fact, no hypnotic suggestions are necessary since the alluring images that are all over are far more manipulative in their summoning for identifications. The role of the image in personality formation and the role of milieu are strong and, as Laing says, "There are endless ways in which a person can be trained to mistrust his own sense."[127]

Such intruding contexts often dictate how each individual should live his or her life. In such contexts--in all contexts?--the individual will always feel alienated from his or her experience which would cause an unbearable state of ambiguity. Often, there is conflict between one and the symbolic order since the individual does not always subscribe to the facts of a certain society because the latter is not necessarily good, especially when the norms of life are not tolerated. Anyone who does not engage in the same system of identifications will be considered an odd outsider or intolerably insane. The patient is by definition in conflict with some cultural premises.

FREEDOM

Since, according to Lacan, the structure of the subject lacks any causality and, thus, it cannot be unalterable, and, as long as the

---

[127]Laing, Self and Others, p. 144.

subject is a system operated by various external and internal agencies that act on many levels, it cannot stay stable or pure. But how freely do the processes that define the structure of the subject operate, how vulnerable and open are they to change and how far does one's freedom to be selective extend? In *Book II,* Lacan says: "... there is nothing random in whatever we undertake with the intention of doing so at random."[128] There is a suspicion that this freedom of choice that selects is an illusion, it has been already determined by unconscious functions that actually prevent one from being free: "In so far as the subject exists... his essential reality consists in the junction of reality and the appearance of tables of presence. That doesn't mean that it's him who creates them all.... The game is already played, the die already cast... with the following proviso, that we can pick it up again, and throw it anew."[129] As long as the structure of a subject is never fully completed or "realized", there is no specific place where one can locate anything, including its freedom. Freedom does not mean spontaneity. There is free choice, yes, but, at its most radical, the choice is a forced one. As in *Oedipus,* the oracle that is uttered before he was born predicts what will happen.[130] In fact, what makes a subject such is the fact that it is subject to a (forced) choice. Although there is nothing inherent except lack, yet, nothing is ultimately free.

Even the freedom attained as a result of the awareness of the symbolic system one lives in does not mean that one is left with many choices. Greater freedom does not mean greater number of options, for there is no autonomous source of activity. In a system of determinism--which does not follow same patterns that have stable

---

[128]Lacan, Book II, p. 188.

[129]Ibid., p. 219.

[130]"Oedipus ... everything happens as a function of the oracle ... the reality of which he is ignorant." Ibid., p. 209.

correlations between the causes and the effects and precise pre-dictions,[131] but which refers to the power one has over the other--the status of consciousness is not that of freedom; there are limits within which one is free and freedom within which one is enclosed. The old Iranian *pairidaeza,* from which the word "paradise" comes--similar to the Greek *peri*--refers to enclosure, wall, something that sets boundaries and limits or protects. Perhaps, true freedom comes after one's realization of one's lack of it, of the passivity and dependence on the Other, the recognition of necessity. As Lacan claims in the *Four Fundamental Concepts of Psychoanalysis,* "The status of the unconscious, which, as I have suggested, is so fragile on the ontic plane, is ethical: in his thirst for truth, Freud says, *Whatever may happen, it is imperative to go there.* "[132] One may not be able to choose one's point of view, but may be able to choose whether to allow oneself to be affected by certain influences. One can only affirm responsibility and suffer the strain of throwing the burden back on one's self. One may not be free only insofar as one misrecognizes the causes that determine him or her.[133]

The only conclusion one could reach is that one deals with a very labyrinthine matter that will stay as such. All the parts and functions of the subject are mingled in a Borromean knot that is as singular as it is complex.

---

[131]"Now, the very idea of determinism is that law is without intention." Book II, p. 295.

[132]J. Lacan, The Four Fundamental Concepts of Psychoanalysis, ed. Jacques-Alain Miller, trans. Alan Sheridan. NY: W. W. Norton, 1978. *The Four Fundamental Concepts of Psychoanalysis, Seminar XI* (1973), N 33.

[133]ŽiŽek "The Cartesian Subject Versus The Cartesian Theater," in Cogito and The Unconscious, p. 270.

7. Analysis

Lacanian psychoanalysis questions the role of therapy and the methods of cure practiced by psychology, and opposes any reduction of psychoanalysis to therapy. It does not adopt the method of diagnosis, prescription and treatment, nor is it a compromise operation that would use the ego as the agent between the reality and pleasure principles, and become the agent of adaptation of the individual to society. One should also be careful in inferring that psychoanalysis is mainly concerned with the human distress and intentions, the subsequent actions and their consequences. For Lacan, therapy is not cure, and analysis is not a kind of *catharsis*-purgation, but these are ways to lead to the awareness and recognition of self-delusions, and the adjustment of the individual to the way things are. The aim of analysis is not the relief from suffering, to be "healthy", for, how "healthy" can a human being be and how can suffering be alleviated, completely and enduringly? As Freud said, psychoanalysis, pedagogy and politics are the three impossible professions.

Lacan reconceptualized the foundations of psychoanalysis on an iconoclastic basis. According to him, the core target and obstacle of an honest analysis are the "ideal" selves. Not unlike Descartes, one has to discard all idealizations, all imaginary "you are thats", until one gets to what one really is, or better, is not, since, unlike Descartes--the champion of certainty--Lacan desubstantializes the subject. The latter is not a psyche that dwells in the body--although it is embodied--nor is it a thinking substance.

In the topos of the Imaginary, one creates oneself and pays a cost one does not know. On the other hand, the unnegotiable cost that would be paid when one discerns the actual relations and patterns that manufacture oneself may also be unbearable. Since the task is not to discover but to disclaim oneself in order to "know oneself"--which means to know an unlikely and baffling identity--the emergence from one's fantasy usually necessitates some kind of violence which one may or may not be able to tolerate. Analysis is painful, it destroys pieces of the ideal ego that constitute one's "self", it is a violent process of de-being, of severing aspects of being, and as such, it cannot occur without tumult, for the critical reflection it requires may not always be pleasant, nor safe.

But, what is it left when one gets rid of all the fictions and frees oneself from all imaginary lures, all mirror captivations? What is it like to be a subject without misrecognitions, unspoiled by the substance of the ego, and what is the kernel in oneself that can survive in isolation from its environment? What is the pure subject prior to subjectivization like? A pure human being, or a monster? And what happens when one sees these identifications critically and tries to untangle oneself from them? What is the ontological, existential, emotional and spiritual cost one has to pay for discerning this truth?

Lacan's answer would be that what remains is purely an empty spot occupied by the subject of enunciation. For being empty, it can be universal, and it can indeed be seen as the form of subjectivity implied by science, a merely formal subjectivity purified of all content and substance.[134] As Žižek explains, "... Descartes's "error", if it can be so called, consists in substantializing this empty spot of *cogito* by turning it into *res cogitans*. Lacan's starting point in this reading of cogito is the assumption that cogito implies, in its pure and minimal form, a non-imaginary subject as a void."[135] The self can be defined only negatively, as no-self, an empty space vulnerable to imaginary invasions; as the inaccessible Thing in Itself, the sublime; as a natural--and thus impossible--subject living in the Real. The place where one's true subjectivity can be situated is somewhere outside the field of anything one can speak about.

---

[134]Dolar, "Cogito as the Subject of the Unconscious," p. 15.
[135]Ibid., p. 16.

Because of the urge for identity and a feeling of continuity and well-being, the psychotic ego is the one that denies its split--the fact that one constitutes one's ego ideal on the model of one's ideal ego--and any change. The psychotic, stuck at the mirror with the illusion of oneness with the mother thinks that s/he lacks nothing and, using rationalizations, displaces blame on others. However, the effect of ideal ego, everything one likes about oneself and as the core of one's being, is alienating. Lacan gives an advice:

> The resistances always have their seat in the ego. What corresponds to the ego, is what I sometimes call the sum of the prejudices which any knowledge comprises and which each of us has as individual baggage. It is something which includes what we know or think we know--for knowing is always in some way believing one knows. On account of that fact, when you are shown a new perspective, in a manner which is decentred in relation to your experience, there's always a shift, whereby you try to recover your balance, the habitual centre of your point of view--a sign of what I am explaining to you, which is called resistance. What you should do, on the contrary, is open your minds to the notions being generated by another domain of experience, and turn it into your own profit.[136]

After the desubstantialization of the subject, the question of what is the aim of psychoanalysis is the point where the Lacanian challenge begins. Lacanian psychoanalysis, unlike ego psychology, is not a normalization technique. Therapy does not consist in the reintegration of the fragments of the self, which have never been a unit on the first place. Psychosis is not a phenomenon of a deficiency, the result of an

---

[136]Lacan, Book II, p. 41.

organic or psychical anomaly, and there is no assumption of a kernel of insanity in mental illness or any definite signs of a paranoid construction. Nor is psychoanalysis the celebration of the unconscious or that of the obscurity of the object.

Psychoanalysis, according to Lacan, is the *theory* of the unconscious. In his hands it became not a system of cure, not a treatment one "applies," but a technique and process of listening to the testimony of one's desire and its recognition. Its aim became the investigation of the self, of the reflective status of one's phenomenal self-awareness and understanding, as well as articulation of one's confusion. The point is to reflect on one's unconscious wishes and their corresponding creations of realities, to be aware of one's fantasies and fictions and to make one's worldview clear. As C. Castoriadis says, "The flux of associations, punctuated by the analyst's interpretations, brings into action the reflexive activity of the patient; he reflects himself and reflects upon himself...."[137] This working through, however, demands constant self-criticism and a mature flexibility, an openness to change. Here Lacan urges for contemplation and meditation and used the following analogy to demonstrate that his teaching was not a dogma but the eroticism of thinking itself:

> The master breaks the silence with anything--with a sarcastic remark, with a kick-start. That is how a Buddhist master conducts his search for meaning, according to the technique of Zen. It behooves the students to find out for themselves the answer to their own questions. The master does not teach ex cathedra a ready made science.[138]

---

[137]Castoriadis, "Psychoanalysis and Politics," p. 5.
[138]Lacan, The Seminar of Jacques Lacan, Book I, p. 1.

Psychoanalysis, as the analysis of the unconscious and not as therapy, is therefore disconnected from medicine.

The transformation one may experience in psychoanalysis by the release from ego ideals and ideal egos, is both a self discovery and a liberation. Analysis provides the awareness that may lead to a reflective life--an end in itself. As he says in *Écrits,* "It is my thesis that psychoanalysis is not merely a particular form of psychotherapy; it is at all times also a philosophy of life."[139]

Unlike the "self-alteration" enterprise of Behaviorism, psycho-analysis is not a technique, but rather a poetics. As in pedagogy, the intention is "not to teach particular things, but to develop in the subject the capacity to learn: learn to learn, learn to discover, learn to invent."[140] One learns to develop the capacity to become autonomous, animated, de-hypnotized, and transformed. The patient becomes the analysand, the one who participates in therapy, in fact, the patient is the main agent of analysis who self-reflects, recalls, re-cognizes, and works through. Lacan, precisely because he wants to free the individuals and make them able to choose, does not strictly specify the objective, precisely because the subjects should develop the ability to make their own statements of preference and select the values which will denote their own choices. Likewise, any new ideas about individuality are connected with new ideas and forms of therapy, yet to be discovered.

The problem in analysis and therapy is not the ignorance but the inner resistance, and the aim is not to "know thyself" but to know the desire, "not to inform but to evoke"[141] and to bring the unconscious dimension of the subject's speech into his or her awareness. Analysis

---

[139]Lacan, Écrits, p. 175.

[140]Castoriadis, "Psychoanalysis and Politics," p. 6.

[141]J. Lacan, Écrits, p. 86.

spots the symptoms that communicate the unconscious and lifts one from the hell of the unrecognized conflicts whose perplexity it describes and it forces one to cope with one's deepest desires and fears. Psychoanalysis is to confront one with one's desire, to restore the analysand to his or her desire that lies unacknowledged within his or her demands. The analyst's task is to get the analysand to answer the question: What is my desire? In the process of resolving a conflict, therefore, one does not elude it, since elusions are like lies, one leading to many others, but seeks a direct confrontation with it. As Freud said, "To tolerate life remains, after all, the first duty of all living beings. Illusion becomes valueless if it makes this harder for us."[142] The result is "one of reintegration and harmony, I could say of reconciliation."[143] In any case, recognizing desire does not mean seeking pleasure--*jouissance* is not synonymous with pleasure, but a form of boundlessness.

Yet, how can one treat an always-veiled desire that never presents itself as such and it can hardly ever be concrete and recognizable, precisely because it is the desire for something one had never really known or possessed? And what if this desire wants to stay desiring, forever resisting any cure? In fact, it always remains unsatisfied, for, there is the necessity of desire, and, as long as it demands symptoms for its gratification, we are all ailing. The subject is defined by its desire and when not desiring it seizes to be: Desidero ergo sum. The Lacanian desidero is the Freudian discontent. Desire will always interrupt the regularities of one's life and psychoanalysis will always stay tragic: there is no reconciliation, no cure, no redemption. Seeing madness as consisting primarily of aggression, Lacan saw that there is

---

[142]S. Freud, <u>The Standard Edition of the Complete Psychological Works of Sigmund Freud</u>, ed. James Strachey. 24 vols., London: Hogarth, 1953-1974, 14. 72, p. 299.
[143]Lacan, <u>Écrits</u>, p. 171.

an impossibility of resolution that does not involve tragic disaster. The analyst does not have the "answer" to one's suffering and one can only try to explain illness but not cure it. There is no such thing as peace of mind. This, however, does not announce the end of psychoanalysis, but its challenge.

Since the iconoclastic desire is commonly "experienced" indirectly-- the Other is discernible in bodily symptoms, speech, life style, etc.-- analysis follows the process of investigation, exposure in words and understanding of one's desire and its relation to one's truth. Because the language of desire is the symptom that "communicates what it does not actually say,"[144] analysis unenvelopes forces, dynamics, structures, intentions, defenses, patterns. Since the unconscious makes its presence felt in language, its focus is the irruptions of unconscious processes into conscious discourse, "the paradox of conceiving that the discourse in an analytic session is valuable only in so far as it stumbles or is interrupted."[145] The symptom, which is structured like a language, like a metaphor, since one signifier replaces another, is resolved when the substitution is uncovered.

In the field of the social and individual situation it is impossible to isolate single causes, thus, for Lacan, who used a holistic model of evaluation, psychosis has no single essence and, therefore, no single cause, but originates in a multiple determination. Since nothing exists outside a context, it emerges out of a life, of one's concrete history and the complicated web of one's relations with the world: with time, space and other people. While nothing is meaningful by itself, through analysis one needs to contextualize one's life and unravel what constitutes one's identifications, networks of references, one's signifieds, those social fictions that structure and determine one's life.

---

[144]Lacan, Écrits, p. 82.
[145]Ibid., p. 299.

Since experience is a later construct based on a mixture of discontinuous perceptions, judgments and so forth, and, since the effects of the "facts" of those events that determine our existence come later in the form of symptoms, analysis, according to Lacan, should examine the history of the subject and determine the events that caused the symptoms that reflect a state in the psychical history of the subject. Analysis' goal is to discern what, in all our histories, insists and resists through the symptoms, and to discover the determinants of the subject's behavior. The unconscious should be understood not on the basis of instincts but of history: "The spoken clarification is the mainspring of progress. The images will take on their meaning in a wider discourse, in which the entire history of the subject is integrated. The subject is as such historisized from one end to the other. This is where the analysis is played out—on the frontier between the symbolic and the imaginary."[146] And since mental illness or health does not depend on one's anatomy, analysis is history. What is effective in analysis is this re-collection of the history, that is, the way one presently perceives and bears one's past, as well as the power, the effect this remembrance has on the subject that is spoken: "What we teach the subject to recognize as his unconscious is his history--that is to say, we help him to perfect the present historization of the facts that have already determined a certain number of the historical "turning points" in his existence."[147] In this respect, psychoanalysis, as the process that elucidates the origin of the split, becomes also a psychosynthesis. By subjectivizing those events, by making them personal and exclusive, one reconstructs one's history, decomposes the personality structure and reconstructs oneself.

But how does one get from here to self-consciousness? According to Lacan, self-consciousness, the "thick moment" of consciousness, the

---

[146]Lacan, Book II, p. 255.
[147]Lacan, Écrits, p. 52.

awareness that "I am now-here-alive", is originally passive. This is in clear contrast to the notion according to which self-awareness originates in the subject's active relationship toward its environment, and to the notion that it is the constitutive moment of one's activity of realizing a determinate goal. What originally one is aware of is that "I am not in control, that my design misfired, that things just drift by. A computer that merely executes its program in a top-down way, for that very reason "does not think", is not conscious of itself."[148] Self-consciousness is the encounter with the Real and the impossible, the process that lets the Other have its say.

Lacan understood therapy also as the interpretation of the relationships of the individual and the community, since one is usually not fully aware of the existence of the social matrix comprised by the cultural values and the communication systems that prevail. He observed an interplay of powerful social forces with internal conflicts, the fluidity of these relationships, and the changes they indeter-minantly may draw. Accordingly, he treated analysis not oriented around the individual, but around one's function as a social being.

The aim of analysis cannot be to make all of the unconscious conscious and to be controlled by rational deliberations, which is an impossible objective, but to make one aware of the forces that repress and their reasons. And since the causality of one's desire is neither only social nor only psychological, but structural, the analysis of the law of one's desire has to be such as well. The problem is not only of the individual but also of the society and the inherent ways of a vicious circle by which it organizes itself, again, based on individual desires. While one may always "experience" what is happening, one is not always aware of it, since the individual has--not superficially--internalized and, perhaps, worshiped the existing institutions, and he or she is not in a situation to realize, to "see" them. Since the ego is

---

[148]Žižek, "The Cartesian Subject Versus the Cartesian Theater," p. 268.

largely a social fabrication that rigidly embodies and reproduces the fixed social institutions that created it, it is necessary to see the individual in the framework of its social situation.

After the realization of the fact that the so far self-evident fictions, what one considered "natural" and "normal", have no substantial actuality, that they are valid but inexistent, one cannot be the same subject as before. To the question if there is something wrong with the world or oneself, the answer is that there is something wrong with both. In any case, the subject has to accept and lament the unbearable lack of the Other. Since its imbalance is constitutive, the subject is always synonymous to its lack and ultimately doomed to fail. One is always at crossroads, and confusion is converted into better-defined conflicts. Expressing one's desire does not guarantee happiness and, as Freud stated, analysis is to change illness into common suffering and the realization that many of the disappointments are ordinary. As Eisner puts it in *The Road to Daulis,* "we simply have to learn to get along as conscious cripples in a society of unconscious cripples."[149]

Although Lacan wanted to restore human dignity, he was against any blind optimism and challenged the view that the mind can be treated or even understood. The fact that to be human is to fail to make the ideal compromise is what makes him tragic. Suffering cannot be redeemed; there are no hiding places, no escapes. Any attempt for a just and caring world is doomed to fail. Yet, he does not give in to despair--while he is also scornful of (self-inflated) heroism. Life is both a curse and a gift. What saves is the *deus ex machina*--a fiction that actually creates more disillusionment. For Lacan what is left to advocate is style, the decency of the ordinary.

---

[149]R. Eisner, The Road to Daulis: Psychoanalysis, Psychology, and Classical Mythology, Syracuse University Press, 1987, p. 31.

To the question of what does a postmodern psychoanalysis that denies any cure mean for one's life, and what happens when there is no hope for medical healing, Lacan holds that the individual has some power on the context it finds itself, some space for creativity and transformation since ambiguity involves openness to various possibilities. Humans live in border zones, between self-determination and the ability to exercise human intelligence to plan and deliberate on the one hand, and divine decrees and the mercy of luck on the other. Humans are still responsible to choose what is important. For Lacans, life itself is an interpretive process that arranges one's world. In *Ethics and Psychoanalysis,* Lacan maintains that with sublimation an object is raised to the unrepresented *(das Ding),* the same way that "Tragedy elevates the object to the dignity of the Thing."[150] Sublimation refers to the dimension of depth in everything. One simply has to change perspective and, paradoxically, perceive the object-- which does not incarnate a self-evident meaning and which is deprived of any identifications, emotions, thoughts--as "insignificant", like the human condition which forms collapses and dissolves into emptiness. Sublimation occurs when death breaks into life and one can see the limits; to live with death in mind. This is what catharsis is: to recognize the Thing without been destroyed.

Lacan values aesthetics over ethics and implies an ethics of aesthetics. Art has an ethical function, and "cure" refers to the greater capacity for sublimation which is based not on an ethics of the sovereign good, but, since the tragic does not necessarily resist the ethical, on tragic ethics and on the ethics of chance--neither prescribes what gives meaning and direction in one's life.[151] His ethics of sublimation is

---

[150]Van Haute, "Death and Sublimation in Lacan's reading of Antigone," p. 117.

[151]However, Lacan claims that "the ethics of analysis do not contradict this (to guide one towards *happiness*) ... otherwise the analysis will amount to little more than a crude suggestion." <u>Écrits</u>, p. 231.

connected to the meaning of the beautiful which affirms life and style, that is, difference, and through which one is "taken away from the present."[152] Psychoanalysis, although it cannot define what is good, is a moral and aesthetic practice that aims to make livelihood a work of art. Living with grace is itself the therapist.

a. The Role of the Analyst

Lacan dictates that the analyst should refuse to act as "a physician, to give diagnosis, to grant a prescription... or to take any decision whatsoever... simultaneously refused to act as a confessor, counselor, or even as a friend."[153] The hope or need that someone else could know for oneself the law of one's own desire proves that there is an integral hesitation or even opposition to know. Since the problem in analysis is not the ignorance but the inner resistances, analysis should deliver one from this resistance as well as lazy confidence to and submissive need for authorities, and alert to the responsibility for acknowledging the truth about one's desire: "The analyst is the man to whom one speaks and to whom one speaks freely. That is what he is there for... they (associations) open up onto a free speech, a full speech, a full speech that is painful to him. Nothing is more to be feared than saying something that might be true."[154] One resists knowing what one suspects and, as Shoshana Felman also observes, psychoanalysis is a pedagogical experience:

> As a process that gives to new knowledge previously denied to consciousness, it affords what might be called a lesson in cognition (and miscognition), an epistemological

---

[152]Louis Althusser, <u>Writings on Psychoanalysis: Freud and Lacan</u>, New York: Columbia University Press, 1996, p. 184, n19.

[153]Althusser, p. 88.

[154]Lacan, <u>Écrits</u>, p. 253.

instruction.... Teaching, like analysis, has to deal not so much with lack of knowledge as with resistances to knowledge.... Ignorance, in other words is nothing other than a *desire to ignore:* its nature is less cognitive than performative.[155]

As long as one's desire is integral in one's choices, one's destinies, histories and lives, who else can know them better than oneself? The analyst is not the agent who will do it for one, for one's understanding of his or her experience can only be indirect; events occurring in other persons are accessible by inference alone. The analyst is definitely not the one who would tell the analysand what and how he or she--always unconsciously--feels, thinks or experiences his or her personal relations and the world. Although the analyst--who should have the mastery of a variety of systems of communication--can rely only on one's accounts and gestures to speculate how one experiences things, he or she cannot escape from a subjective way of perceiving, defined by his or her values.[156] There are differences of systems of value and their codification, and there are circumstances and states of being that the others (including the analyst) may not be aware of. Since the world is possibly never experienced by two individuals in the same way, we do experience it differently, and, in a sense, we live in different worlds. Not only might this puzzle the analysand, but there is also the risk of offense and of the loss of trust to the discipline. As Laing also says, "One person investigating the experience of another can be directly aware only of his own experience of the other. He cannot have direct awareness of the other's experience of the "same" world.... All one "feels", "senses", "intuits", etc. of the other entails inference from

---

[155]S. Felman, Jacques Lacan and the Adventure of Insight: Psychoanalysis in Contemporary Culture, Cambridge: Harvard University Press, 1987, p. 76, 79.
[156]Ruesch and Bateson, p. 11.

one's own experience of the other to the other's experience of one's self."[157] Direct examination is impossible and listening is the only investigational technique. Nonetheless, the analysts's role is important, for the social system cannot be observed directly, but only by the experience of contrast.

Analysis may count on free association, yet, this should also be a carefully regulated arrangement. As the organizer of the investigation and like a Zen Master, the analyst must coordinate the sessions discretely, keep a close control of the process and remove the limitations of self-observation. The analyst does not have to be exceptionally wise, nor should he or she be a Good Samaritan:

> What appears here as the proud revenge of suffering will show its true face--and sometimes at a moment decisive enough to enter the "negative therapeutic reaction" that interested Freud so much--in the form of that resistance *of amour-propre...* and which is often expressed thus: "I can't bear the thought of being freed by anyone other than myself"... it is the hostile reaction that guides our prudence, and which inspired Freud to be on his guard against any temptation to play the prophet. Only saints are sufficiently detached from the deepest of the common passions to avoid the aggressive reactions to charity.... In any case, such reactions should hardly surprise us analysts; after all, do we not point out the aggressive motives that lie hidden in all so-called philanthropic activity?[158]

The analyst will not take the role of a god and save one either from the illusions one lives in or from the illusion of the existence of a state

---

[157]Laing, Self and Others, p. 21.
[158]Lacan, Écrits, p. 13.

without them. For Lacan, it would have been the worst of illusions to aspire for his analysands a state of a total absence of illusion, for a lack of illusion would suggest no desire yearning for a fulfilment. As it has been demonstrated, Lacan recognized the structure of the self in new terms and turned psychoanalysis from an instrument of cure to one of recognition. His effort was to save one from the semantic traps, that is, of the imaginary, and the analysand has to realize that even analysis-- in its orthodox form--is itself part of its structures. As J. Gallop also says, "Every psychoanalytic critic has a transference onto psycho-analysis, that is, a belief that psychoanalysis is the site of a "knowledge of meaning."[159]

Both the analyst and the analysand are parts of a larger social system that is also the immediate concern to psychoanalysis. The analysand is not an object under observation, but both the object and the subject of investigation; and so is the analyst who also belongs to a symbolic order. The analyst's concept of health is not the point of reference. As Julia Kristeva says, "Each analysis modifies--or should modify--at least some of the beliefs about psycho-dynamics that I held before hearing what the analysand had to say."[160] Each subject's desire--as the product of his or her particular structural histories and arrangements (and not only of the social or psychological ones)-- makes a particular "case."[161] Since desire will always be tentatively disclosed and understood, both analysand and analyst are under constant training, and psychoanalytic concepts and techniques are permanently under construction: "If it is true that our knowledge comes to the rescue of the ignorance of the analysand, it is no less true that we, too, are plunged in ignorance, insofar as we are ignorant

---

[159]Gallop, Reading Lacan, p. 29.

[160]J. Kristeva, In the Beginning was Love: Psychoanalysis and Faith, trans. Arthur Goldhammer, New York: Columbia University Press, 1987, p. 51.

[161]Lacan, Book I, p. 12.

of the symbolic constellation underlying the unconscious of the subject."[162]

The analyst should also apply neutral listening. Although conflict may set a threat to social discourse, the analyst should not condemn the analysand's fantasy and impose or even suggest another social fantasy system. An authoritarian therapist who conceives himself as the representative of society is not interested in the solution of conflicts. The analyst does not function as a physician who may represent social control, but as a guide. The analyst should refuse to play the role of the authority that prescribes what one should be and what one should do. His or her role is not to know, dominate and control, but to potentiate, to motivate, and insist on experiences that the analysand denies and suppresses. It is not the analyst's task to deny the way the analysand is seeing and experiencing the world, because psychoanalysis, unlike other psychological methods and practices, is a process affirming responsibility. Since madness may be partially automatic, stemming from elsewhere, and partially intentional, the analysand should become more responsible about the choices he or she makes and how he or she sees and experiences the world. One should become aware of oneself as well as confident of one's powers.

Since each individual is unique and the concept of normality or deviation cannot be sufficient, then, training in psychiatry would be futile since no generalizations can be made. As a consequence, the analyst loses his/her position as expert, that is, as the authoritative therapist, for how can one cure a pathology that structures human development after all? There can be no guarantee of where analysis will lead, no assurance of normality. Refusing to adhere to any reductionist model, Lacan himself did not consistently maintain any view of life, and he thought that at the end of the analytic session one

---

[162]Lacan, Seminar I, p. 178-79.

should know that no one could know. Finally, the analyst must follow the fate of the Other: he or she, as any master, must be abandoned and finally replaced.

b. Transference

Lacan also recognized that to comprehend fully a situation one has to become participant and acquire a personal experience, yet, he also acknowledged the limitations of self-observation and the need to objectivize distance in transference. The transference or identification with the analyst is both psychologically unsettling and effective, since the proper distance it sets avoids denials. The analyst insures a balance between conflicts and security, between in and out, engaged and detached, thought and feeling. There is deep emotional resonance, but also a feeling of control.[163]

The analytic session should create systems of desire and identification, that is, a space for transference, which will facilitate the awakening of the unconscious, the surfacing of fundamental fantasies and the rearticulation of the analysand's desire. Transference is a temporary method of treatment, the reenacting and reworking of relations and attitudes that have been suppressed and which, this time, are directed to the analyst-- whose role is "not to inform but to evoke"[164]--and to bring the unconscious dimension of the subject's speech into his or her awareness. Through the relation of love or hate for the analyst, the analysand acquires a distance from the ego and becomes aware of ego fictions.

Žižek holds that the analyst is not a dialogical partner, not another subject, but the object a.[165] Analysis establishes a relation

---

[163]T.J. Scheff, Catharsis in Healing, Ritual, and Drama, University of California Press, 1979, p. 64.

[164]Lacan, Écrits, p. 86.

[165]Žižek, "A Hair of the Dog That Bit You," in Lacanian Theory of Discourse, p. 46, 60.

of the subject to his shadowy double, the externalized object in himself, the empty mirror, the absolute Other.[166] The face of the analyst is blank, there is no truth behind it, and the third gaze sees what is in himself more than himself. It is not the ego talking to an alter, rival ego but rather a subject talking to a radical other, the Other:[167] "What one seeks in transference, in an other, is the Real, one's truth articulated in desire, it is "a movement *from reality to the Real*."[168] This is what, according to Lacan, has to be accomplished in the analytic process by working through the transference. He also states:

> Analysis is becoming the relation of two bodies between which is established a phantasmic communication in which the analyst teaches the subject to apprehend himself as an object.... The subject begins... the analysis by speaking about himself without speaking to you, or by speaking to you without speaking about himself. When he can speak to you about himself, the analysis will be finished.[169]

Transference is connected to the state of collusion in which, according to Laing,[170] one desperately seeks for relationships which

---

[166]"Analysis progresses through the speech of the subject in so far as it passes beyond the dual relation, and thus no longer encounters anything except the absolute Other...." Lacan, Book II, p. 270.

[167]Gallop, Reading Lacan, p. 107.

[168]Žižek, "Why is *Woman* a Symptom of Man?" p. 55.

[169]Lacan, Écrits, p. 91, 106.

[170]"The term 'collusion' has kinship with de-lusion, il-lusion, and e-lusion. Lusion comes from the verb *ludere,* whose meaning varies in classical and late Latin. It can mean to play, to play at, or to make sport of, to mock, to deceive. Delusion implies total self-deception. Illusion, as frequently used psychoanalytically, im-

will endorse the false notions of one's self. Lacanian transference, in order to succeed in its real purpose, should function as the process that frustrates such yearning as much as possible. Lacan says:

> If I frustrate him (the speaker) it is because he asks me for something. To answer him, in fact... his demand is intransitive, it carries no object with it... demand to cure him... a radical demand.... Thus the analyst is he who supports the demand... in order to allow the signifiers in which his frustration is bound up to reappear.[171]

The analyst should refuse the analysand's demand of love and the analysand should become aware that transference is a signifier, "a relationship... to what one lacks in one's self knowledge and thus loves in the other." As Laing also agrees, "The therapist's intention is not to allow himself to collude with the patient in adopting a position in their phantasy-system, and, alternatively, not to use the patient to embody any phantasy of his own."[172] Suffering is the very state of mind that assumes and desires an answer that has been intentionally concealed and, paradoxically, the intensification of the frustration of this assumption and desire is the answer. One of the reasons Lacan stopped his sessions abruptly was precisely to disturb the expectation

---

plies a capacity to deceive oneself under a strong wish, but does not involve self-deception as total as delusion. Collusion has resonances of playing at and of deception. It is a 'game' played by two or more people whereby they deceive themselves. The game is the game of mutual self-deception ... each plays the other's game, though he may not necessarily be fully aware of doing so. An essential feature of this game is not admitting that it is a game." R. D. Laing, Self and Others, p. 90.

[171]Lacan, Écrits, p. 255.

[172]Laing, Self and Others, p. 105.

for collusion and frustrate the analysand who might expect that the analyst would comply to his or her longing.

Although the aim of analysis is to make one aware of one's false identifications, paradoxically, the analysis of the unconscious is founded exactly on this, on transference, the intersubjectivity between analysand and analyst. As J. Gallop observes, analysis produces imaginary effects (transference, projection of images), but its goal is to understand what structures those effects. This makes it apparent that the Symbolic could be accessed only through the Imaginary. Analysis is a cure of idolatry by idolatry and, as J. Kristeva says, "What today's analyst must do, I think, is restore to illusion its full therapeutic and epistemological value."[173] J. Gallop agrees that, founded on transference, analysis refers to the dissolution of fantasies in a homeopathic way:

> The symbolic can be reached only by not trying to avoid the imaginary, by knowingly being in the imaginary. Likewise, mastery of the illusions that psychoanalysis calls transference can be attained only by falling prey to those illusions.... In the ethical imperative to be in the symbolic, the charge is to look into the mirror and see not the image, but the mirror itself.... It is the imaginary as imaginary which constitutes the symbolic... the repetitive insistence of (infantile) desires in the transference and their permanent recollection in a signifier where the repressed returns... a desire must insistently repeat itself until it is recognized... thus repetition is the effect not so much of the frustration of a desire but of the lack of recognition of a desire.[174]

---

[173]Kristeva, p. 21.
[174]Gallop, <u>Reading Lacan</u>, p. 59 62, 104.

Since, according to Lacan, the truth of the self is always already alienated and madness is irreducibly inherent in the world, he recognizes the irreducibility of fictions and, thus, the necessity of illusion that, in the individual as well as the community, is part of the necessity of things. Lacan claimed: "Models are very important. Not that they mean anything--they mean nothing. But that's the way we are--that's our animal weakness--we need images... it is rather the symbolic deficiency which is worrisome."[175]

Psychoanalysis and Ethics

In the 50s, the psychologist Lewis S. Feuer wondered if the values of liberal civilization are strengthened or undermined by the methods of psychoanalysis, if ethical philosophy disintegrates under analysis.[176] One can respond that ethics and psychoanalysis are not mutually exclusive and that ethics is not impossible. Psychoanalysis does not exclude ethics; the loss of identity that Lacan describes does not irredeemably confuse one's ethical role.

A contemporary analysis of social and cultural forms cannot ignore psychoanalytic insights and it is imperative that one rethinks ethics through psychoanalysis, indeed, as lying at the heart of it. Any such implications would prove the ethical core of it and recognize what Žižek says Lacan was doing all the time: "Reading hysteria or obsessional neurosis as a philosophical "attitude of thought towards reality."[177] There is a need to explore the religious and ethical

---

[175]Lacan, Book II, p. 88.

[176]Samuel L. Feuer, Psychoanalysis and Ethics, Springfield: Charles C. Thomas, 1955, p 3.

[177]Slavoj Zizek, "Introduction: The Censure of the Speculative," in Speculations After Freud: Psychoanalysis, Philosophy and Culture, ed. Shamdasani, Sonu and Michael Munchow. New York: Routledge, 1994, p. 2.

implications of Freud's and Lacan's revolution in thought, to explore how one could incorporate the Lacanian exploits into a speculation about life and one's relations with others and the world, one's fundamental recognition of desire and desire for recognition.

An important implication of the Lacanian psychoanalysis is the fact that the individual identity has faded, that the origins of the true self, this inaccessible other, became irretrievable; there is an other, a lack at the very heart of the self. This repressed otherness that refers to the forces that shape the unconscious and which can never be fully symbolized, now becomes the structuring principle of subjectivity. This loss of identity, however, does not irredeemably confuse one's ethical role.

According to Lacan, the subject cannot imagine anything outside the imaginary. This fact--that one constructs and develops the notion of who one is and that one desires to create a self when no original self exists--prompts the question of the very possibility of epistemology.

Following the above, how can (the no-thingness of?) the self establish the foundation for all thought? Apparently, this (no-thingness of the?) self cannot ground a presupposition of all thought. This Lacanian scrutiny of the truth of the subject provokes the examination of its relation to knowledge and truth. The redefinition of the self calls for the redefinition of knowledge, truth, and ethics as also processes and constructs of relations. Who has the authority to claim knowledge now? One may conclude that for Lacan subjectivity and knowledge refer to the same thing; they both are "effects", constructs, an economy of relations, products relative to context rather than producers, impossible positive existences. Lacan separates truth from knowledge in a new radical way. The subject is an embodied discourse structure, socially constituted by knowledge. Since knowledge is rooted in errors, there can be no progressive advance of it; it will always be incomplete and the "truth" will always be inaccessible.

It follows that, since we construct and develop our selves and as long as subjectivity stays unfinished and open ended, its intellectual and theological implications will also stay unfinished, undecided, open to various possibilities and accessible to interventions. In *The Four Fundamental Concepts of Psychoanalysis,* Lacan states that, "Desidero is the Freudian Cogito."[178] This again yields the crucial complication: How can the nothingness of the desiring self establish the foundation for all thought, and how could one facilitate this incapacity to know in the study of Religion? Since God belongs to the unknowable and unutterable Real, how can one have any sincere theological discourse?

There is certainly a need to re imagine ethics. The Lacanian model of the developing subject--variable, interacting, perpetually becoming and open-ended--provides the foundation for rethinking Ethics as a similarly open ended orientation. There is a need to give an ethical meaning to Desire, the insatiable yearning for something that can never be found, "the desire for nothing."[179] There is no destination, no prediction, no utopia. There is a need for an ethics free from repression, that is, an uncompromising and honest ethics that takes desire seriously since desiring is what makes one human. However, humans are insatiable beings and their desire, omnipotent and unfulfillable, constantly persecutes them. There is a need for ethic's self-critique and for a self-definition as an inquiry, as a safeguard against compliance, as a searching and questioning, as a psychoanalytic and ethical odyssey.

Ethics is to renounce dogmatic views, since no unified theory is possible as long as it occupies a space in the structure of the unconscious. It should not be thought as an imperialism that preaches the exclusivity of a closed system and lures to welcome beliefs that have nothing to do with people's experiences of themselves, although they regulate them. A Postmodern ethics that which acknowledges the

---

[178]Lacan, The Four Fundamental Concepts of Psychoanalysis, p. 154.
[179]Lacan, The Seminar of Jacques Lacan, Book II, p. 211.

Other, the unthinkability of the unthought can no longer be "systematic." Having no referent, it stays hypothetical and heuristic, as if in search of an answer. Tentative and incomplete, it leads to other modes of discourse, different types of knowledge and ways of thinking. Being uncommitted, flirtatious and perpetually seduced by the unknown, it makes uncertainty erotic. Invariably affirming the otherwise, it creates polylogs, plateaus that hold tension and keep heterogeneity unresolved, frustrating any climax and generating only aporias; as such, ethics can only be a nonperfectionist *Spiegel spielen,* the delight, the *eros* of the experience of critical thought,[180] the piety of thinking itself. It is a quest.

Lacan's insistence on the priority of difference over sameness reflects an ethical quality of psychoanalysis. In order to enter the symbolic, the subject has to recognize, relate to and respect the other as other, in spite of the fact that its desire for the other will remain ever unsatisfied. Mature human relations should not deny the object its own being. This is the major challenge faced by each person in the course of development: to learn to relate to others as genuinely other. This maturity refers to the awareness of the reciprocal effects of communicative actions and of the beneficial effects of successful human relations.[181]

The fact that there is no such thing as self-mastery goes along with the fact that there is no self-sufficiency either. One actualizes one's life, one "exists" only when one co-exists, when one matters and gratifies his or her need to affect and to make a difference to the other. This is why people who do not know where they belong--the

[180]J. Rajchman, Truth and Eros: Foucault, Lacan, and the Question of Ethics, New York and London: Routledge, 1991, p. 1-10.
[181]J. Ruesch and G. Bateson, Communication: The Social Matrix of Psychiatry, p. 89.

borderline ones--suffer from a feeling of non-being. As Mark Taylor also says, "In negating the other, the self finally negates itself."[182]

This notion of selfhood, therefore, contradicts any isolating individualism. The subject is a social, a "political animal," and rejection, or simply the fear of it, brings frustration and despair. One demands *re-cognition*, confirmation that one exists and that this makes a difference, a place of significance in another's world. As J. Gallop says, Lacan's writing contains an "implicit ethical imperative to break the mirror," to disengage, loosen, unbind from the Imaginary and enter the Symbolic, the register of language and social exchange. What is ultimate, here, is how one decides to make one's "epochal arrangements" based on what one thinks is important, and how one negotiates life in relation to others.

The effect of Lacanian discourse is to promote individual as well as social engagement, for the unbearable pain of lack demands connection and comfort in companionship, the development of associations with others. To recognize and be recognized, to give and receive praise, become imperative. Since the self is defined by its actions and its relations with others, the individual affair is also a public issue. One's fate is linked, and, therefore, one needs to be public spirited. Good refers to the socially responsible sublimations, while relatedness to others itself has therapeutic effects.

Although analysis, according to Lacan, has a social basis and functions, yet, it does not point to a crude socialization or a collectivism in which the sentiment of responsibility disappears.

The ethical implications of such a psychoanalysis cannot be restricted to an ethical or moral *attitude of tolerance* of the idiosyncrasies of others, to a "belonging *together*." Ethics is not simply the moral "aspect" of Lacan's psychoanalysis, but an orientation and a dimension of depth that pervades it entirely. It is more than ethical, it

---

[182]Mark C. Taylor, Erring: A Postmodern A/theology, p. 32.

is a *"belonging* together," precisely because the subject's orientation is interactive and open-ended, rather than originary and self-enclosed.[183]

Yet, the need for recognition is infinite, and the desire for confirmation of one's presence and importance cannot reach total fulfillment, since one is always uncertain and moves between trust and mistrust, confidence and despondency. The need for a genuine interhuman life and the assurance that one is worthy of love is and will remain tragic; it will be repeatedly spoiled by the suspicion of the other's pretense. Further, some relations of love and sympathy, some strong attachments, may in fact be narcissistic identifications since, when one extends oneself, one may fail or simply refuse to distinguish him or her from an object. Since, in such cases, relations are identifications and the world is not clearly distinguished from the self, they are also "mad". Lacan sends one in search of another to complement oneself; it is not only the psychotic who seeks a literal image of himself or herself. Only when one notices and distinguishes the difference between things is also when one becomes aware of them, and also aware of one's self and its ways. As Gregory Bateson says, "... only where there is difference between two persons in contact is it possible for those persons to achieve a new understanding, a new awareness of the previously unconscious premises which underlie their own habits of communication."[184]

Still, if only subjective realities exist, as according to Lacan, how does one know about the particulars of each other's experience except by verbal communication? If there is no such thing as objective reality out there, talking, that is, communicating, is the only way for establishing strong communities of relatedness. And, since language functions as communication as well as non-communication, in order to be

---

[183]James DiCenso, "Symbolism and Subjectivity: A Lacanian Approach to Religion," in The Journal of Religion 74, January 1994: p. 45-64.

[184]Ruesch, Jurgen and Gregory Bateson, Communication, p. 229.

able to approach the other, communicative competence is needed as well as the avoidance of distorted interpersonal and intrapersonal communication. If it is true that, "the condition which the psychiatrist labels "psychosis" is essentially the result of the patient's misinterpretation of messages received,"[185] and that psychopathology is unsuccessful or disturbed communication, one needs to protect one's "sanity" by improving communication within oneself and with others. Communication requires to speak well.

For Lacan, culture itself is based on speech and everything is played out in language. Language is "the matrix in which all human activities are embedded"[186] and human relations can be developed only through it. As Bateson also says, thinking is "constituted from the outside world and returns through the symbolic, in words, in images--any action constitutes a message,"[187] and "the study of knowing... is inseparable from the study of communication, codification, purpose, and values. We have thus modified the study of epistemology towards the inclusion of a specific range of external phenomena...."[188]

However, problems lie in the fact that there are different habits of communication and a lack of a system common to all. The fact that "a signifier is that which represents a subject... not for another subject, but for another signifier" means that the subject cannot be like a sender transmitting a message to a receiver. This implies that the translation of one's language into another's, as well as the possibility of communication, is fundamentally problematic. According to Lacan, there can be no dialogue, no real exchange between two individuals, but only a juxtaposition of monologues.

---

[185]Ibid., p. 88.
[186]Ibid., p. 13.
[187]Ibid., p. 34.
[188]Ibid., p. 228.

Nevertheless, even if it communicates nothing, the discourse represents the existence of communication:[189] "Henceforth the decisive function of my own reply appears, and this function is not, as has been said, simply to be received by the subject as acceptance or rejection of his discourse, but really to recognize him or to abolish him as subject. Such is the nature of the analyst's *responsibility* whenever he intervenes by means of speech."[190] As ŽiŽek also holds, speech is the medium of the mutual recognition of the speakers and of human relatedness.[191]

Insisting on the significance of verbal communication and prompting the recognition of the existence of other people with different, even opposing desires, Lacan professed engagement in cultural dialogues, global pluralism, tolerance and generosity. Precisely because there can be no fixed center or identity, there can also be no single symbolic structure and worldview, but multiple modes of human experience of reality. Lacan provided the frame for an intended diversity and, by doing so he opened a cultural debate, a critical inquiry that marked the collapse of previous modes of thinking. One has no choice but to affirm and celebrate the way things are, the difference of meanings, without taking any sides, an attitude which can also apply to a new way of understanding human and social relations which, believing in the individual and not in a collective being, maximizes originality, idiosyncrasy, style. As long as people are equal but different, none has to look alike.

Still, one has to be very careful how one reads the ethics of social exchange, for it can imply exactly the opposite of what it means to say. Like A. Zupancic,[192] one may wonder what exactly the commandment

---

[189]Lacan, Ecrits, p. 43.

[190]Ibid., p. 87.

[191]ŽiŽek, "A Hair of the Dog That Bit You," in Lacanian Theory of Discourse, p. 46.

[192]A. Zupancic, "The Subject of the Law," in Cogito and The Unconscious, ed. Slavoj ŽiŽek. Durham and London: Duke UP, 1998, p. 43.

would be: to respect the difference of the other, or the other has the right to be different? To tolerate, or, to love? Even further, should one tolerate or love the ones who do not respect difference? Or should one "kill all the fanatics"? When he discussed, in the *Civilization and its Discontents,* the commandment "Thou shalt love thy neighbor as thyself," which in Lacanian language would correspond with the register of the imaginary, Freud himself saw that it was easy to fall into a conventional morality, based not as much on genuine humanitarian compassion as on a personal insecurity and narcissistic self-love. In *Ecrits,* Lacan comments:

> ... the term primary narcissism... throws light on the dynamic opposition between this libido and the sexual libido, which the first analysts tried to define when they invoked destructive and, indeed, death instincts, in order to explain the evident connection between the narcissistic libido and the alienating function of the I, the aggressivity it releases in any relation to the other, even in a relation involving the   most Samaritan of aid.[193]

He concludes: "For such a task, we place no trust in altruistic feeling, we who lay bare the aggressivity that underlies the activity of the philanthropist, the idealist, the pedagogue, and even the reformer."[194] In the *Ethics of Psychoanalysis,* Lacan detected that "it is a fact of experience that what I want is the good of others in the image of my own. That doesn't cost so much. What I want is the good of others provided that it remains in the image of my own."[195] The crucial question is whether one should show respect only if the other is good, which means the same. In the same Seminar, Lacan added another conflict:

---

[193]Lacan, Ecrits, p. 6.

[194]Ibid., p. 7.

[195]J. Lacan, The Ethics of Psychoanalysis, 1959-1960: The Seminar of Jacques Lacan: Book VII, ed. J-Alain Miller. Norton & Company, 1992, p.187.

My neighbor possesses all the evil Freud speaks about, but it is no different from the evil I retreat from in myself. To love him, to love him as myself, is necessarily to move toward some cruelty. His or mine? you will object. But haven't I just explained to you that nothing indicates that they are distinct? It seems rather that they are the same, on condition that those limits which oblige me to posit myself opposite the other as my fellow man are crossed.[196]

J.-A. Miller sees the delicacy of the examination of the social and ethical implications of Lacan's theory and the danger of taking his assertion too lightly and naively and of falling into the same fallacy of the fanatic enemy. In "Extimite," Miller talks about the Other as the neighbor and discerns the gaps and discrepancies in Lacan himself. He wonders if the difference is cultural, or more important and fundamental: "But if there is no Other of the Other what is the ground of his alterity?" He concludes:

... It is in its relation to *jouissance* that the Other is really Other... Now, what we are attempting to see is what makes the Other other, that is, what makes it particular, different, and in this dimension of alterity of the Other, we find war. Racism, for example, is precisely a question of the relation to an other as such, conceived in its difference. And it does not seem to me

---

[196]Ibid., p. 198. While Lacan urged the recognition of the existence of other people with different, even opposing, desires, he also pointed to that of the Other within: "Moreover, it is not simply the *jouissance* of the neighbor, of the other, that is strange to me. The kernel of the problem is that I experience my own *jouissance* as strange, dissimilar, other, and hostile ... one cannot think the radical otherness ... without stumbling against the problem of the Same."

that any of the generous and universal discourses on the theme of "we are all fellow beings" have had any effectiveness concerning this question. Why? Because racism calls into play a hatred that is directed precisely toward what grounds the Other's alterity, in other words, its *jouissance.* If no decision, no will, no amount of reasoning is sufficient to wipe out racism, this is indeed because it is founded on the point of extimacy of the Other... racism is founded on what one imagines about the Other's *jouissance;* it is hatred of the particular way, of the Other's own way, of experiencing *jouissance.* We may well think that racism exists because our Islamic neighbor is too noisy when he has parties. However, what is really at stake is that he takes his jouissance in a way different from ours. Thus the Other's proximity exacerbates racism: *as soon as there is closeness, there is a confrontation of incompatible modes of jouissance. For it is simple to love one's neighbor when he is distant, but it is a different matter in proximity* (italics mine). Racist stories are always about the way in which the Other obtains a *plus-de-jouir:* either he does not work enough, or he is useless or a little too useful, but whatever the case may be, he is always endowed with a part of *jouissance* that he does not deserve. Thus true intolerance is the intolerance of the Other's *jouissance.* Of course, we cannot deny that races do exist, but they exist insofar as they are, in Lacan's words, races of discourse, that is, traditions of subjective positions.[197]

Zupancic also agrees that a Lacanian ethics should be re-formulated from the perspective of *jouissance,* rather than from the perspective of the sharing of one's goods.[198] Psychoanalysis steps into

---

[197]J.A. Miller, "Extimite," in <u>Lacanian Theory of Discourse: Subject, Srtucture, and Society</u>, p. 79-80.

the field traditionally reserved for ethics precisely because it deals with *jouissance,* the Real, the impossible, the frequently designated as the Evil.

Lacan's ethics, whose main problem lies on the narcissistic self-deception, is related to the challenges of how to teach analysis and how to change the individual and alleviate suffering. Ethics must not be based on obligation or politics, but on desire.[199] At his *Seminar on The Ethics of Psychoanalysis,* delivered in 1959-60, he said: "And it is because we know better than those who went before how to recognize the nature of desire, which is at the heart of this experience [the loss of the mother], that a reconsideration of ethics is possible, that a form of ethical judgment is possible, of a kind that gives this question the force of a Last Judgment: Have you acted in conformity with the desire that is in you?"[200]

As in Freud, it is a moral obligation to restore human dignity to the human condition, for the Cartesian subject, with the asceticism of reason and the obsessive compulsion to think--"if I stop thinking, I will cease to exist"--*is* a monster.[201] The dream of rationalism that

---

[198]Zupanic, "The Subject of the Law," in Cogito and the Unconscious, p. 42.

[199]Aristotle relates ethics with politics. In his Nicomachean Ethics, he says: "Most people would regard the good as the end pursued by that study which has most authority and control over the rest. Need I say that this is the science of politics?... This is not to deny that the good of the individual is worthwhile. But what is good for a nation or a city has a higher, a diviner, quality. Such being the matters we seek to investigate, the investigation may fairly be represented as the study of politics." Ethics: Book I. Trans. J. A. K. Thomson, New York: Penguin, 1953, p. 26-27.

[200]Lacan, The Ethics of Psychoanalysis, p. 314.

[201]Žižek, "Introduction," p. 6.

perceived reason as ultimate is an antihumanism that reduces the self to cogito and, thus, betrays human nature and announces "the death of man." The Cartesian subject is the excess of the cogito, a hubris in itself and, as Castoriadis said, "... analysis is thereby explicitly opposed to all ethics based on condemnation of desire and therefore on guilt."[202] As part of a culture--an agreed upon system of preferences and a set of exchanges and criteria for action--the concepts of ethics are historically restricted. Ethics usually has to do with systems of value, and its codes are the result of pressure from groups that prescribe the standards of human behaviour and put pressure to conform and blend into the group reinforcement of prevailing cultural values. According to Freud, there is nothing metaphysical about one's values. One always has a certain reason to guard them. Anything that is culturally determined such as norms and values has a functional purpose; it provides a version of reality and the source and justification of actions. Besides, the fundamental paradox of ethics lies in the fact that, in order to found an ethics, one already has to presuppose a certain ethics, that is, a certain notion of the good. Yet, precisely because they are culturally determined, that is, of human origin, ethics are circumstantial, and, therefore, fragile and vulnerable, and as long as there are multiple ways of conceptualising truth, there are as many ways of conceptualising ethics, too.

An important observation that Freud made was that there is a "discontent" precisely because the "good" principles one honours are false or illusory. They are not supreme but, indeed, they are symptoms of one's discontent, the products of one's sublimations, that is, one's

---

[202]Cornelius Castoriadis, "Psychoanalysis and Politics," in Speculations After Freud: Psychoanalysis, Philosophy and Culture, ed. Shamdasani, Sonu and Michael Munchow. New York: Routledge, 1994, p. 4.

attempt to deal with scornful desires such as aggressivity. Lacan insisted that finding out about one's unconscious desires and motives is an ethical obligation. Commenting on Lacan's propositions, John Rajchman wrote: "To return to Freud was to return to these embers in the convent of psychoanalysis. It was to say again what psychoanalysis is, should be, had never stopped being despite its misconceptions of itself: a new ethic."[203]

There are also other forces--besides the moral law--that drive one to act against one's well-being. Lacan insisted that psychosis itself, as the denial of one's desire and one's clinging to the symbolic order, has ethical determinants. If there should be one faith, it is the faith in the unconscious. As J. Kristeva said there is a desire not to know, as if to know means to suffer.[204] There is a fear of loss, of the void of emptiness at the centre of being, and one tries to keep the ground from shifting. To achieve this, one would idealize objects and false cures and do what the analyst wishes, the latter's desire being important. Madness is this refusal of responsibility and is a way to relate to the lack, to the lack of lack. None can ignore the implications of Oedipus' ignorance whose sanity depended on it, yet, by not knowing, he committed incest and a plague ruined his city and everyone around him. The unconscious may be a merciless barbarian, but it may also be an intelligent and benevolent deliverer. In fact, one can enjoy no peace until one faces and better understands one's own unconscious sources. Lacan urges one to do so, since desire is so powerful that this task cannot be neglected.

There is a need to reconsider ethos and "... discover the connection

---

[203]Rajchman, Truth and Eros, p. 21.
[204]Julia Kristeva, "Psychoanalysis in Times of Distress," in Speculations After Freud, p. 16.

between ethics and "pathos,"[205] and aspire to the balance of truth and *jouissance*.[206] In Ecrits, Lacan says:

> An ethic is yet to be formulated that integrates the Freudian conquests in the realm of desire: one that would place in the forefront the question of the analyst's desire... analysts on the whole imagine that to understand is an end in itself, and that it can only be a "happy end". The example of the physical sciences may show them, however, that the greatest successes do not require that one knows where one is going. To think, it is often better not to understand, and one can gallop through miles of understanding without the least thought being produced. This, indeed, was how the Behaviourists began: they gave up the attempt to understand....[207]

Yet, the questions remain. How can one base one's ethics on a desiring causality, on what desire decides to do? How can one organize and foresee one's life on the basis of this kind of "beyond"? The question of how one can speak truly of oneself has both epistemological as well as ethical implications, raising the philosophical problem of truth as well as of life. The reconceptualization of subjectivity, along with its ethical implications, interrogates the very possibility of epistemology and demands the reconceptualization of knowledge as well, in this case the knowledge of what is good. Paradoxically, by choosing to acknowledge epistemic undecidability, one also chooses responsibility for an ethical decidability: "In the recourse of subject to subject that we preserve, psychoanalysis may

---

[205]Rajchman, Truth and Eros, p. 31.
[206]Kristeva, "Psychoanalysis in Times of Distress," p. 19.
[207]Lacan, Ecrits, p. 252.

accompany the patient to the ecstatic limit of the "Thou art that", in which is revealed to him the cipher of his mortal destiny, but it is not in our mere power as practitioners to bring him to that point where the real journey begins."[208] J.-P. Vernant agrees that, "The tragic consciousness of responsibility appears when the human and divine levels are sufficiently distinct for them to be opposed while still appearing to be inseparable. The tragic sense of responsibility emerges when human action becomes the object of reflection and debate, while still not being regarded as sufficiently autonomous to be fully self-sufficient."[209] Lacan says: "... the question of responsibility is raised on the subject of a crime somewhat lacking in motivation... by not underlining the responsibility of the person in question, he himself may once again open up the door on to a general massacre."[210]

The questions "how to best live one's life" and "how can one live successfully" demand immediate answers. Since ethics refers to a way of life, there is a demand for an ethical response, an ethical responsibility and commitment in everyday life. Yet, in a world of capricious and incomprehensible powers, how should one live? Lacan thought that, "if God doesn't exist, then nothing at all is permitted any longer."[211]

When an indeterminate number of random fragments replaced a simple, closed, mechanical "self," it became hard to imagine what it would be like to look down upon the subject and find it good. As soon as the subject became the temporary result of interactions between arbitrary environmental pressures and limitations, it could no longer teach one how to live, for, how could a product of dubious social

---

[208]Ibid., p. 7.
[209]Jean-PierreVernant, and Pierre Vidal-Naquet, Myth and Tragedy in Ancient Greece, Trans. Janet Lloyd, New York: Zone, 1988, p. 27.
[210]Lacan, Book II, p. 208.
[211]Ibid., p. 128.

relations and capricious symbolic orders, instruct, set beliefs and demand that one acts with prediction? If one cannot know oneself, restricted by ontology, how would one expect to decide what is good and how would one set any ideals and live a life based on idealized values? As Zupancic says, there is nothing that can help us guess.[212] As in the case of health, there is great skepticism about who decides whose good is more valuable and about what one's ethical duty is. Ethics cannot be based on good. Zupancic concludes that,

> The Freudian blow could be summarized as follows: what philosophy calls the moral law and, more precisely, what Kant calls the categorical imperative, is in fact nothing other than the superego... to base ethics on "pathological" foundations... "civilization and its discontents." As far as it has its origins in the constitution of the superego, ethics is nothing more than a convenient tool for any ideology that tries to pass off its own commandments as authentic, spontaneous, and "honourable" inclinations of the subject.[213]

In any case, the complication of Lacanian ethics is not how to find what is good for each and everyone, rationalize it and then adopt it. His psychoanalysis is beyond good and evil. Its aim is not to make a good individual, at least not directly. Neither does he provide any behavioural model. He declares: "I am not engaging you in an *ex cathedra* teaching. I don't think it would befit our object, language and speech, for me to bring something apodictic for you here, something you must just have to record and put in your pocket."[214]

---

[212]Zupancic, "The Subject of the Law," p. 56-57.

[213]Ibid., p. 41.

[214]Lacan, Book II, p. 291.

According to Lacan, although the subject is not the agent of its actions, it is responsible for what one refers to as one's duty. For him duty is founded only in itself, which allows for the freedom and responsibility of the moral subject. His ethics do not equal virtue and morality[215] based on universalist categories, paradigms of behaviour, rules and laws, since desire is not universal but particular and specified. His ethics is not a way of judging but a way of thinking. ŽiŽek attempts to describe the way Lacan would define an authentic ethical act: "Therein consists the Lacanian definition of the ethical act: an act which reaches the utter limit of the primordial forced choice and repeats it in the reverse sense. Such an act presents the only moment when we are effectively "free": Antigone is "free" after she has been excommunicated from the community. In our time, such acts seem almost unthinkable: their pendants are usually disqualified as "terrorism."[216]

The pertaining question is directed to the amount of choice one has in constituting oneself and in regulating one's life. Desire, not intention is what really is at work within, directing one's fates. The

---

[25]"... if the neurotic is like a private or asocial moral agent, a moral agent is a public, socialized neurotic. If obsession, hysteria and paranoia are like distorted pathological versions of ourselves as moral beings, our images of ourselves as moral beings are like idealized versions of these pathological conditions. And the principle that thus connects duty and pathology, the principle that says that there is no duty without pain is this: our desire is so structured by the Law as to make of us "obligated" or "guilty" sorts of beings *before* we formulate just what our obligations or duties are, and the principles that would govern them. Such would be the great Freudian reversal in morality: we don't repress our desire because we have a conscience; we have a conscience because our desire is always and already repressed." in Rajchman, Truth and Eros, p. 41.

[216]ŽiŽek, "Why Is Every Act a *Repetition*?" in Enjoy Your Symptom, p. 77.

Other decides for us, without us, instead of us. Where the Other reigns there are no causes and effects operating in a mechanistic way and there can be no planned decisions. Desire, the result of absence and lack, is the master of the house. Since desire is always repressed, what one may think that one wants for oneself may not actually coincide with one's desire. It is not reason that makes one autonomous. As in therapy, the aim is not to get better control of one's self and life, but to have insight into one's own inauthentic choices in creating one's self, to analyse one's values, to learn how to be satisfied and to become capable of happiness.

Psychoanalysis does not teach the meaning of one's existence and life; as Cornelius Castoriadis says, it can only "help the patient to find, invent and create for himself such a meaning... to form his own project for life"[217] and achieve the maturity of the liquidation of illusions and the denial of imaginary fascinations, a maturity that "always involves knowledge of the relativistic value of the meaning of things."[218] It does not aim at social adaptation through inhibition and repression, but at the release from repression from social constructs. Its aim is not a struggle against desire (as traditional moralities dictate, although such a restraint may be seen as a way to gratify it), but against the suffering that breeds defense in the form of illusions and, eventually, more suffering. As Deleuze says,[219] what forces one to think is always a violence, in this case, the violence of one's conflicts and symptoms, the experience of some malfunctioning, of some perturbation. Life rises to consciousness when there is pain and one is ready for change when life becomes unbearable.

---

[217]Ibid., p. 10.

[218]Ruesch and Bateson, p. 87.

[219]G. Deleuze, Difference and Repetition, Columbia University Press, 1968, p. 139.

According to Lacan, therefore, psychoanalysis has an ethical objective: it should help the individual to recognize the fact that he or she participates in a certain symbolic order, since one's self-understanding is facilitated by a new insight into the symbolic values, those social fictions that structured and determined one's life. The recollection of free association exposes and elucidates the symbolic system one lived in when experiencing certain traumatic events, and assists one's awareness of the symbolic system that determines the present. One acquires a new perspective and notices the oddness of what is going on. Since madness could be defined as the degree of the ambiguity created by the conflict of one's reality with that of the social system and the extent to which one can endure it, the role of analysis is also to make one aware of this ambiguity and, in certain cases, the treatment would be a modification of one's life situation. The subject's health does not depend on any *adjustment* but on the *willingness or ability to conform,* that is, to reconcile to the world in which it finds itself, or on the willingness and ability to move to a different environment, to reorganize one's relations and reshape one's identity:

> There is a symbolic circuit external to the subject, tied to a certain group of supports, of human agents, in which the subject, the small circle which is called his destiny, is indeterminately included.... Naturally, the subject can spend his entire life without making out what it's about. It is after all what most commonly happens. Analysis is made for him to make out, for him to understand in what circle of speech he is caught, and by the same token into what other circle he must enter.[220]

---

[220]Lacan, Book II, p. 98-9.

Communities: A Place for Identity and Difference

What makes one reality more socially acceptable than the other? What determines what will prevail in a specific time and place? The time and place themselves? And what happens when the last two factors are ignored, and a community adopts the intriguing reality of someone else who lives under totally different circumstances? Then there is the clash of two worlds. There is crisis when the Other does not make sense, when its lack appears, when the Symbolic domain can no longer hold the subject.

In Lacan, the Other can be irregular and inconsistent since it does not exist without the human community; in fact, the actual human world is what constitutes it. As everything that is specifically human, it is the "as if" that holds a community together and guarantees the consistency and ultimate meaning of its subjects' experience. But is this "as if" a lie, a necessary illusion, or an unintended compromise, and who are the ones who need to be deceived and why? Yet, if it is an intended lie, and since the liar deceives without deceiving himself, then, the "as if" is not a deception; it is a play, a *ludere,* Nietzsche's "metaphysical comfort."

The subjects presuppose but also pose the Other,[221] they are both the authors and the aftermaths. Individuals are both an effect and an ingredient of the symbolic--we are the creators of significance, and societies are badly unified sets of means that can secure no subordination to them. As J. Hillman says, communities are "constituted of communal contingencies."[222] Freud wondered whether the living being's fundamental tendency is to conserve or to expand, and he introduced the notion of process: The self is not a structure but a process, and the normal is not static. Life depends on development,

---

[221]Zizek, "Why Is *Woman* a Symptom of Man?" p. 59.
[222]Hillman, "Man is by Nature a Political Animal," in <u>Speculations After Freud</u>, p. 35.

variation, mutations, and inventions, and many of today's truths will become yesterday's. There are no powerful invariants. The changing components belong to a wider system which itself is undergoing continual transformations. Cultures constitute themselves, they do not derive from any metaphysical, mythological, theological realm and,[223] as W. C. Greene says, all periods are transitional: "Now the same event will appear variously as cause, as incident, or as result...."[224] As in Heraklitus, there is a primacy of change in everything (concepts, values, "reality") and the urge to recognize the inescapable, universal-- social and individual--flowing, transitions, transformations, renewals, is strong. The symbolic remains open to constant change and the whole world, in order to assure survival, is subject to the open-endedness of mutations, that is, variations of the same. Nothing assures that one cannot reverse oneself and turn into its opposite, that, in fact, it does not already contain its opposite.

The Other should not be maintained at any cost, unless there is a historical necessity fulfilling a noble mission, a meaning. Lacan would guide people to break the order of security and regularity. New communities should withdraw from the Other, decompose its structure, renounce any support in it and abandon it, risking being accused of madness. They should transform thought, decompose human knowledge and evacuate, empty, restructure and replace it with alternatives. Something else has to bear the burden of the signifying mechanism. Value (from the word *valere*, which means to be in good health, that is, not only comply with but also create values and to decide what has value, what are the things that make life worth living), is what makes a human life good.

---

[223]S. Shamdasani, "Introduction: The Censure of the Speculative," in Speculations After Freud, p. 1.
[224]Chase William Greene, Moira: Fate, good, and Evil in Greek Thought, New York: Harper and Row, 1944, p. 90.

But, being in a vast landscape and tormented by the anxieties of multiple choice and lack of direction, one is seduced to dismiss or neglect change or transformation and to settle for any known set of identifications, and cling to cherished pathological relations, illusions and their misery. There will always be a longing for stability and security; there is no life whatsoever without norms, and an engagement in a community of trust and commitment is crucial. In an all-permitting world there are many possibilities for development but also a need for frameworks, limits within which to order life. Some falsifications are needed. There is a need for objectives and customs that would order life. In order to survive, a community must have planning for the future, driving aspirations, points of reference, collective values, identity. It needs principles, some con-promises to guide action based on the respect for both difference and identity. One cannot constantly proceed with a suspended step, going out of step. There is need for some predictability. It is not always wise to abandon the old for the new and there will always be a longing for stability and security. The opposite of autihumanitarianism should not be anarchy and there is a need to construct social ethics and loyalties that are not based on ethical imperatives. But how can a community that will suffer from no repression be established, and how should people administer and conduct their activities and live together with overlapping truths? In a culture of plurality of values there are inevitable conflicts, but are cultural disagreements and differences in ethics irreducible? In fact, antagonisms are welcome, and one can simultaneously hold incompatible beliefs since as Lacan claims, "Reality is defined by contradiction."[225] In such cases there can be no hierarchy of different knowledges, since there is no absolute one. Community offers the space for a play of identity and difference. Criticism should not be an attack, eristic, a strife, a quarrel, and the

---

[225]Lacan, Book I, p. 267.

dominant one should learn by its defeated rivals. Conflicts between different options, choices and freedoms, tensions, disagreements, and confrontations are inevitable and, therefore, there should be some arrangements to contain aggression. Since not all possibilities are to be realized, and since none should be allowed to forbid what one does not like, there is a need for agreement. According to a Greek myth, Zeus sent *aidos* and *dike* as the virtues that would protect communities and individuals from unrestrained selfishness and guard civilization and order. In cultures of rich diversity any reconciliation or equilibrium always rests on interplays of conflict and tensions among differing modalities of thought, various sensitivities, different experiences. As individualism should not be confused with individuality,[226] conflict does not necessarily mean incompatibility, and opposed truths and conflicting perspectives can be parallel and complementary. Any set of terms should remain provisional and open to intervention. Lacan suggests to "blow alternatively hot and cold." Since there are no lasting changes, there should be an interplay of constancy and change. The idea of *nomos* is not wrong, but it is incomplete.

The opposite of a selfish individualism should not be an intrusive communism and a horrendous homogeneity. Communities should be based on a culture of relationships, that is, communities that want to listen. The social efficacy of language and speech is its *peitho* (persuasion), and there is a need of *Sevas* (respect), not by force but by persuasion whose medium is language, verbal skill--not, however to be used to make the worse appear the better, since persuasion is not rhetoric. Values are, therefore, preferred channels of "communication or relatedness."[227]

---

[226]As M. Taylor puts it, "In the very struggle to achieve distinction by standing a-part from the other selves, the individual eventually comes to realize an unavoidable commonality, which grows out of inevitable relationships with others." in Erring, p. 132.

[227]Ruesch and Bateson, p. 8.

Bibliography

Althusser, Louis. Writings on Psychoanalysis: Freud and Lacan. New York: Columbia UP, 1996.

Archard, David. Consciousness and the Unconscious: Problems of Modern European Thought. London: Hutchinson and Co., Ltd., 1984.

Arrive, Michel. Linguistics and Psychoanalysis: Freud, Saussure, Hjelmslev, Lacan and Others. Trans. Lames Leader. Philadelphia: John Benjamins, 1992.

Bar, Eugene. "Understanding Lacan." Psychoanalysis and Contemporary Thought 3 (1974): 473-544.

—. Semiotic Approaches to Psychotherapy. Bloomington: Indiana UP, 1975.

Borch-Jacobsen, Mikkel. Lacan: The Absolute Master. Trans. Douglas Brick. Stanford: Stanford UP, 1991.

Bronstein, Zelda. "Psychoanalysis without the Father." Humanities in Society 3.2 (1980): 199-212.

Bychowski, Gustav. Psychotherapy of Psychosis. New York: Grune & Stratton, 1952.

Canguilhem, Georges. The Normal and the Pathological. Trans. Carolyn R. Fawcett. New York: Zone Books, 1989.

Casey, Edward S. "Presence and Absence: Scope and Limits." Review of Metaphysics 139 (1982): 557-76.

Certeau, Michel de. Heterologies: Discourses on the Other. Minneapolis: U of Minnesota P, 1986.

Chaitin, Gilbert D. "Lacan's Return to Freud," Salmagundi 106/107 (Spring/Summer 1995): 307-8.

Chrzanowski, Gerard. "Participant Observation and the Working Alliance." Journal of the American Academy of Psychoanalysis 7 (1979): 259-69.

Cogito and the Unconscious. Ed. Slavoj Zizek. Durham and London: Duke UP, 1998.

Cooper, David. "Who is Mad Anyway?" New Statesman 16 (June 1967): 844-45.

Copjec, Joan. Read my Desire: Lacan Against the Historicists. Cambridge, Massachusetts: The MIT P, 1994.

Crownfield, E., Raschke, C., and Wyschgrod E., eds. Lacan and Theological Discourse. State U of New York P, 1989.

De Waelhens, Alphonse. Schizophrenia: A Philosophical Reflection on Lacan's Structuralist Interpretation. Trans. W. Ver Eecke. Duquesne Studies, Philosophical Series 35. Pittsburgh: Duquesne UP, 1978.

Dean, J. Carolyn. The Self and Its Pleasures: Bataille, Lacan, and the History of the Decentered Subject. Ithaca and London: Cornell UP, 1992.

Deleuze, Gilles. Difference and Repetition. NY: Columbia UP, 1968.

DiCenso, James, "Symbolism and Subjectivity: A Lacanian Approach to Religion," in The Journal of Religion 74 (January 1994): p. 45-64.

Dolto, Francoise. Unpublished Notes. June 16, 1936.

Dor, Joel. The Clinical Lacan. Ed. Judith Feher Gurewich. New Jersey: Jason Aronson Inc., 1997.

—. Introduction to the Reading of Lacan. Northvale, New Jersey: Jason Aronson Inc., 1997.

Duruz, Nicolas. "The Psychoanalytic Concept of Narcissism, Part I: Some Neglected Aspects in Freud's Work." Psychoanalysis and Contemporary Thought 4 (1981): 3-34.

Eisner, Robert. The Road to Daulis: Psychoanalysis, Psychology, and Classical Mythology. Syracuse UP, 1987.

Ellenberger, Henri. The Discovery of the Unconscious: The Evolution of Dynamic Psychiatry. New York: Basic Books, 1970.

Federn, Paul. Ego Psychology and the Psychoses. NY: Basic Books Inc., 1952.

Felman, Shoshana. Jacques Lacan and the Adventure of Insight: Psychoanalysis in Contemporary Culture. Cambridge: Harvard UP, 1987.

—. "On Reading Poetry: Reflections on the limits and Possibilities of Psychoanalytic Approaches." The Literary Freud: Mechanisms of Defense and the Poetic Will. New Haven: Yale UP, 1980. 119-48.

—. "The Originality of Jacques Lacan." Poetics Today 2 (1980-81): 45-57.

—. "Psychoanalysis and Education: Teaching Terminable and Interminable." Yale French Studies 63 (1982): 21-44.

—. Writing and Madness: Literature, Philosophy and Psychoanalysis. Ithaca: Cornell UP, 1985.

Feuer, L. Samuel, Psychoanalysis and Ethics. Springfield: Charles C. Thomas, 1955.

Freud, S., The Standard Edition of the Complete Psychological Works of Sigmund Freud. ed. James Strachey. 24 vols. London: Hogarth, 1953-1974, 14. 72.

Fine, Reuben. "Toward an Integration of Psychoanalysis and the Social Sciences." Psychological Reports 41 (1977): 1259-68.

Forrester, John. The Seductions of Psychoanalysis: Freud, Lacan and Derrida. Cambridge: Cambridge UP, 1990.

Foucault, Michel. The Birth of the Clinic: An Archaeology of Medical Perception. Trans. A. M. Sheridan Smith, New York: Vintage, 1975.

Freud, Sigmund. The Standard Edition of the Complete Psychological Works of Sigmund Freud. Ed. James Strachey. 24 vols. London: Hogarth, 1953-1974.

Gabriel, Yiannis. "The Fate of the Unconscious in the Human Sciences." Psychoanalytic Quarterly 51.2 (1982): 246-283.

Gallop, Jane. Reading Lacan. Ithaca: Cornell UP, 1985.

—. The Daughters of Seduction: Feminism and Psychoanalysis. Ithaka, NY: Cornell UP, 1982.

Gardner, Sebastian. "Splitting the Subject: An Overview of Sartre, Lacan and Derrida." Auslegung: A Journal of Philosophy 10.1/2 (1983): 57-64.

Gilman, Sander. Difference and Pathology: Stereotypes of Sexuality, Race, and Madness. Ithaca: Cornell UP, 1985.

Goux, Jean-Joseph. Symbolic Economies: After Marx and Freud. Trans. Jennifer Curtis Gage, Ithaca: Cornell UP, 1990.

Greene, Chase William, <u>Moira: Fate, good, and Evil in Greek Thought</u>, New York: Harper and Row, 1944.

Grossberg, Lawrence. "The Ideology of Communication: Post-Structuralism and the Limits of Communication." <u>Man and World</u> 15.1 (1982): 83-101.

Grotz, Elizabeth. <u>Jacques Lacan: A Feminist Introduction</u>. New York: Rutledge, 1990.

Habermas, Jurgen. <u>The Philosophical Discourse of Modernity</u>. Cambridge: MIT, 1987.

Hartman, Geoffrey. "Psychoanalysis: The French Connection." <u>Psychoanalysis and the Question of the Text</u>. Ed. Geoffrey Hartmen. Baltimore: Johns Hopkins UP, 1978.

Hegel, G. W. F. <u>Phenomenology of Spirit</u>. Oxford: Clarendon, 1977.

Holloway, Robin. "Jacques Lacan: Language as Foundational of the Unconscious." <u>Issues in Language: Studies in Honor of Robert J. Di Pietro</u>. Ed. Marcel Danesi. Lake Bluff, Ill.: Jupiter. (1981): 135-47.

Ingleby, D. "The Ambivalence of Psycho-Analysis." <u>Radical Science</u> 15 (1984): 39-71.

Kerrigan, William. "Terminating Lacan." <u>The South Atlantic Quarterly</u> 88.4 (Fall 1989): 993-1009.

Kohut, Heinz. <u>How Does Analysis Cure?</u> Ed. Arnold Goldberg. Chicago: U of Chicago P, 1984.

Kristeva, Julia. <u>In the Beginning was Love: Psychoanalysis and Faith</u>. Trans. Arthur Goldhammer. New York: Columbia UP, 1987.

Lacan, Jacques. <u>De la Psychose paranoiaque dans ses rapports avec la personnalite</u>. Paris: Seuil, 1975.

—. <u>Ecrits: A Selection</u>. Trans. Alan Sheridan. New York: W.W. Norton, 1997.

—. <u>Le Seminaire, livre XVII: L'Envers de la psychanalyse: 1969-1970</u>. text etabli Jacques-Alain Miller, Paris: Seuil, 1991.

—. <u>Le Seminaire: livre VIII: L' Ethique de la psychanalyse: 1969-1950</u>. Ed. Jacques-Alain Miller, Paris: Seuil, 1986.

—. <u>Le Seminaire de Jacques Lacan, livre XX: Encore, 1972-1973</u>. texte etabli par Jacques-Alain Miller. Paris: Seuil, 1975.

—. The Seminar of Jacques Lacan: Book I: Freud's Papers on Technique, 1953-1954. Ed. J.-Alain Miller. New York: Norton, 1988.

—. The Seminar of Jacques Lacan, Book II: The Ego in Freud's Theory and in the Technique of Psychoanalysis, 1954-55. Ed. Jacques-Allain Miller. NY: Norton, 1988.

—. "Some Reflections on the Ego." International Journal of Psycho-Analysis 34.11-17 (1953).

—. Speech and Language in Psychoanalysis. Trans. Anthony Wilden. Baltimore: The John Hopkins UP, 1981.

—. The Ethics of Psychoanalysis, 1959-1960: The Seminar of Jacques Lacan: Book VII. Ed. J-Alain Miller. 1992.

—. The Four Fundamental Concepts of Psycho-Analysis. Ed. Jacques-Alain Miller. Trans. Alan Sheridan. NY: Norton, 1981.

—. The Language of the Self: The Function of Language in Psycho-analysis. Ed. and Trans. Antony Wilden. Baltimore: John Hopkins UP, 1968.

Lacan and Narration: The Psychoanalytic Difference in Narrative Theory. Ed. Robert Con Davis. MLN 98.5 (1983): 843-1063.

Lacanian Theory of Discourse: Subject, Srtucture, and Society. Ed. Bracher, M., Marshall W. Alcorn Jr., Ronald J. Corthell, and Francoise Mas-sardier-Kenney. NY: New York UP, 1994.

Laing, Ronald David. The Divided Self. New York: Pantheon, 1969.

—. Self and Others. Tavistock, 1969.

Laplanche, Jean, and J. B. Pontalis. The Language of Psychoanalysis. Trans. Donald Nicholson-Smith. London: Hogarth, 1973.

—. Life and Death in Psychoanalysis. Trans. Jeffrey Mehlman. Baltimore: The John Hopkins UP, 1976.

Laether, Phil. "Desire: A Structural Model of Motivation." Human Relations 36.2 (1983):109-22.

Leavy, Stanley A. "The Rules of the Game." Contemporary Psychoanalysis 21 (1985): 1-17.

Lemert, Edwin McCarthy. Human Deviance, Social Problems, and Social Control. Englewood Cliffs, NJ: Prentice-Hall, 1967.

Levenson, Edgar A. "Changing Concepts of Intimacy in Psychoanalytic Practice." Contemporary Psychoanalysis 10 (1974): 359-69.

—. "Language and Healing." Journal of the American Academy of Psychoanalysis 7 (1979): 271-82.

—. "The Aesthetics of Termination." Contemporary Psychoanalysis 12 (1976): 330-42.

Levinas and Lacan: The Missed Encounter. Ed. Harasym, Sarah, State U of New York P, 1998.

Lotringer, S. "The 'Subject' on Trial." Semiotexte 1.3 (1975): 3-8.

Lyotard, Jean-Francois. "The Dream Work Does Not Think." Trans. Mary Lydon. Oxford Literary Review 6.1 (1983): 3-34.

MacCabe, Colin, ed. The Talking Cure: Essays in Psychoanalysis and Language. New York: St. Martin's, 1981.

MacCannel, Juliet Flower. Figuring Lacan: Criticism and the Cultural Unconscious. London, Croom Helm, 1986.

—. "Oedipus Wrecks: Lacan, Stendhal, and The Narrative Form of the Real." Modern Language Notes 98.5 (1983): 910-40.

Macey, David. "Fragments of an Analysis: Lacan in Context." Radical Philosophy 35 (1983): 1-9.

—. Lacan in Contexts. London: Verso, 1988.

Malcolm, Janet. "Therapeutic Rudeness." New York Times Book Review 3 (April 1983):1, 17-18.

Mancall, Mark. "The Cultural Revolution: Man's Struggle for Liberation." Journal of International Affairs 23 (1969): 132-39.

Mannoni, Octave. "A Brief Introduction to Jacques Lacan." Transl. I. Ilton and A. H. Feiner. Contemporaty Psychoanalysis 8.1 (1971): 97-106.

Masling, Joseph, ed. Empirical Studies of Psychoanalytical Theories. Vol.1. The Analytic P, 1983.

May, Todd. Reconsidering Difference. The Pennsylvania State UP, 1997.

May, Rollo, ed. Existential Psychology. New York: Random House, 1969.

McKenna, Ross. "Jacques Lacan: An Introduction." The Journal of the British Society for Phenomenology 7.3 (1976): 189-97.

Miller, Jacques-Alain. "Ethics in Psychoanalysis." Lacanian Ink 5 (1991): 13-27.

Moloney, Robert. "Knowledge of Self and of Others." Heythrop Journal 17 (1976): 309-21.

Montrelay, Michele. "On Folding and Unfolding: An Example of Dream Interpretation in Analysis." Psychoanalytic Inquiry 4 (1984): 193-219.

Morris, Wesley. "The Irrepressible Real: Jacques Lacan and Post-structuralism." American Criticism in the Poststructuralist Age. Ed. Ira Konigsberg. Michigan Studies in the Humanities, Ann Arbor: U of Michigan. (1981): 116-34.

Muller, Helene. "Another Genesis of the Unconscious." Lacan Study Notes 5 (1985): 2-22.

Muller J. P. and William J. Richardson. Lacan and Language: A Reader's Guide to Ecrits. New York: International UP Inc., 1982.

Muller, John P. "The Analogy of the Gap in Lacan's Ecrits: A Selection." The Psychohistory Review 8.3 (1979): 38-45.

—. "Cognitive Psychology and the Ego: Lacanian Theory and Empirical Research." Psychoanalysis and Contemporary Thought 5 (1982): 257-91.

—. "Ego and Subject in Lacan." The Psychoanalytic Review 69.2 (1982): 234-240.

—. "Lacan's Mirror Stage." Psychoanalytic Inquiry 5.2. pp 233-52.

—. "The Psychoanalytic Ego in Lacan: Its Origins and Self-Serving Functions." Psychological Perspectives on the Self 3. Ed. Jerry Suls and Anthony Greenwald. Hillsdale, New Jersey: Lawrence Erlbaum Associates. (1986): 79-106.

Nehamas, Alexander. "The Rescue of Humanism." The New Republic 203.20 (November 12, 1990): 20-34.

Ogden, Thomas. Projective Identification and Psychotherapeutic Technique. New York: Jason Aronson, 1982.

Payne, Michael. Reading Theory: An Introduction to Lacan, Derrida, and Kristeva. Blackwell, 1993.

Ragland-Sullivan, Ellie. Jacques Lacan and the Philosophy of Psychoanalysis. Chicago: U of Illinois P, 1987.

—. Essays on the Pleasures of Death: From Freud to Lacan. Routledge, New York, 1995.

J. Rajchman, Truth and Eros: Foucault, Lacan, and the Question of Ethics, New York and London: Routledge, 1991.

Rendon, Mario. "Structuralism in Psychoanalysis." American Journal of Psychoanalysis 39 (1979): 343-51.

Richardson, J. William. "Psychoanalysis and the God-Question." Thought 6.240 (March 1986).

—. "The Mirror Inside: The Problem of the Self." Review of Existential Psychology and Psychiatry 16.1/2/3 (1978-79): 95-112.

—. "Lacan's View of Language and Being." The Psychoanalytic Review 69.2 (Summer 1982): 229-233.

Ricoeur, Paul. Freud and Philosophy: An Essay on Interpretation. Trans. Denis Savage. New Haven: Yale UP, 1970.

—. The Symbolism of Evil. Trans. E. Buchanan. Boston: Beacon, 1967.

Roth, Michael. Psycho-Analysis as History: Negation and Freedom in Freud. Ithaca: Cornell UP, 1987.

Rotmiler de Zentner, Maria Ines. "The Identification and The Ideal." Papers of the Freudian School of Melbourne. (1981): 103-118.

Roudinesco, Elizabeth. Jacques Lacan. Trans. Barbara Bray. New York: Columbia UP, 1997.

Ruesch, Jurgen and Gregory Bateson. Communication: The Social Matrix of Psychiatry. New York: W. W. Norton &Company, 1951.

de Saussure, F. Course in General Linguistics. Ed. C. Bally and A. Riedlinger. Trans. W. Baskin. New York: McGraw-Hill, 1966.

Schneiderman, Stuart. Jacques Lacan: The Death of an Intellectual Hero. Cambridge: Harvard UP, 1983.

—. ed. Returning to Freud: Clinical Psychoanalysis in the School of Lacan. New Haven: Yale UP, 1980.

—. "Afloat with Jacques Lacan." Diacritics 1.2 (1971): 27-34.

Schwab, Gabriele. "Genesis of the Subject, Imaginary Functions, and Poetic Language." New Literary History 15 (1983/84): 453-74.

Scott, Charles E. "The Pathology of the Father's Rule: Lacan and the Symbolic Order." Thought 61.240 (March 1986).

Smith, Joseph, ed. Pragmatism's Freud: The Moral Disposition of Psychoanalysis. Baltimore: the Johns Hopkins UP, 1986.

—. ed. Psychiatry and the Humanities. Vol.1. New Haven: Yale UP, 1976.

—. ed. The Literary Freud: Mechanisms of Defense and the Poetic Will. New Haven: Yale UP, 1980.

Smith, Joseph H., and William Kerrigan. Interpreting Lacan, Psychiatry and the Humanities. Vol. 6. New Haven: Yale UP, 1983.

Snell, Bruno. The Discovery of the Mind: The Greek Origins of European Thought. Translated T. G. Rosenmeyer, Cambridge: Harvard UP, 1953.

Speculations After Freud: Psychoanalysis, Philosophy and Culture. Ed. Shamdasani, Sonu and Michael Munchow. New York: Routledge, 1994.

Szasz, Thomas S. The Manufacture of Madness. Dell, 1970.

—. Cruel Compassion: Psychiatric Control of Society's Unwanted. New York: Wiley, c1994.

Taylor, Charles. Sources of the Self. Cambridge: Harvard UP, 1989.

Taylor, Mark, C. Erring: A Postmodern A/theology. Chicago: The U of Chicago P, 1984.

Turkle, Sherry. Psychoanalytic Politics: Freud's French Revolution. New York: Basic Books, 1978.

—. "The New Philosophy and the Agony of Structuralism: Enter the Trojan Horse." Chicago Review 32.3 (1981): 11-28.

Vernant, Jean-Pierre, and Pierre Vidal-Naquet, Myth and Tragedy in Ancient Greece, Trans. Janet Lloyd, New York: Zone, 1988.

Watson, James R. "The Ego and the Other." Tijdschrift vor Filosofie 38 (1976): 574-60.

Webb, Eugene. "The New Social Psychology of France: The Heritage of Jacques Lacan." Religion 23 (1993): 61-69.

Whyte, Lancelot Law. The Unconscious Before Freud. New York: St Martin's, 1978.

Wilden, Anthony. System and Structure: Essays in Communication and Exchange. London: Tavistock, 1972.

Wolpe, J., Andrew Salter and L. J. Reyna eds. The Conditioning Therapies: a Challenge in Psychotherapy. Holt, Rinehart and Winston Inc., 1964.

Wulff, Erich. "Psychoanalysis — A Science of Control?" International Journal of Politics 7.4 (1977-78): 65-92.

Zizek, Slavoj. Enjoy Your Symptom: Jacques Lacan in Hollywood and Out. New York: Routledge, 1992.